Wilhelm Müller's Lyrical Song-Cycles

UNC | COLLEGE OF ARTS AND SCIENCES
Germanic and Slavic Languages and Literatures

From 1949 to 2004, UNC Press and the UNC Department of Germanic & Slavic Languages and Literatures published the UNC Studies in the Germanic Languages and Literatures series. Monographs, anthologies, and critical editions in the series covered an array of topics including medieval and modern literature, theater, linguistics, philology, onomastics, and the history of ideas. Through the generous support of the National Endowment for the Humanities and the Andrew W. Mellon Foundation, books in the series have been reissued in new paperback and open access digital editions. For a complete list of books visit www.uncpress.org.

Wilhelm Müller's Lyrical Song-Cycles
Interpretations and Texts

ALAN P. COTTRELL

UNC Studies in the Germanic Languages and Literatures
Number 66

Copyright © 1970

This work is licensed under a Creative Commons CC BY-NC-ND license. To view a copy of the license, visit http://creativecommons.org/licenses.

Suggested citation: Cottrell, Alan P. *Wilhelm Müller's Lyrical Song-Cycles: Interpretations and Texts*. Chapel Hill: University of North Carolina Press, 1970. DOI: https://doi.org/10.5149/9781469657240_Cottrell

Library of Congress Cataloging-in-Publication Data
Names: Cottrell, Alan P.
Title: Wilhelm Müller's lyrical song-cycles : Interpretations and texts / by Alan P. Cottrell.
Other titles: University of North Carolina Studies in the Germanic Languages and Literatures ; no. 66.
Description: Chapel Hill : University of North Carolina Press, [1970] Series: University of North Carolina Studies in the Germanic Languages and Literatures. | Includes bibliographical references.
Identifiers: LCCN 73635053 | ISBN 978-1-4696-5723-3 (pbk: alk. paper) | ISBN 978-1-4696-5724-0 (ebook)
Subjects: Müller, Wilhelm, 1794-1827 — Criticism and interpretation.
Classification: LCC PT2436.M7 Z85 | DCC 831/ .6

Contents

INTRODUCTION	1
Chapter	
I. Die schöne Müllerin	8
II. Die Winterreise	35
III. Frühlingskranz aus dem Plauenschen Grunde bei Dresden	69
IV. Wilhelm Müller's Poetic Imagination	95
Polarity and Balance	96
The Middle Position	100
The Heart as Lens of the Soul	103
The Poet in the Service of the Spirit	104
The Wellspring of Intuition	106
APPENDIX	115
Die schöne Müllerin	117
Die Winterreise	135
Frühlingskranz aus dem Plauenschen Grunde bei Dresden	147
NOTES	158
BIBLIOGRAPHY	165
INDEX OF FIRST LINES AND TITLES OF POEMS	168

For Oskar Seidlin

Introduction

The poet Wilhelm Müller (1794-1827), famed in his lifetime for his verse in celebration of the cause of Greek independence, lives on in our times largely through the song-cycles "Die schöne Müllerin" and "Die Winterreise," set to music by Schubert. A number of these poems have long since established themselves as popular folksongs ("Das Wandern ist des Müllers Lust," "Am Brunnen vor dem Tore"), while the identity of their author has largely been forgotten. They have come to be felt by the public to be folk poetry, in the popular sense of poetry through which the "soul of the nation" speaks. Similarly, a number of drinking songs by Müller ("Das Essen, nicht das Trinken, / Bracht' uns um's Paradies," "Ich bin nicht gern allein / Mit meinem Glase Wein") today bear the same mark of near anonymity.

The two Schubert song-cycles have maintained themselves among the most beloved of the German *Lieder* repertoire. The usual conclusion drawn from this happy circumstance, however, is that the works have maintained their fame not through any particular merit of the *poems*, but rather through the fact that a great musician was able to breathe life into relatively dead material. There is no question but that Müller's works abound with clichés, conventional imagery, and motifs drawn from all manner of sources ranging from Italian popular poetry[1] to the *Wunderhorn*.[2] At the same time, however, many of the poems are of the most lilting musicality and show a naïve and original manner of expression which cannot be accounted for simply in terms of a dilettante's juggling of conventional themes. It is perhaps most of all this curious mixture of the trite and the spontaneous, the conventional and the unique which has caused the poems to have been largely passed over by literary research.[3] It surely poses a formidable problem for the investigator, who must sift the material cautiously and seek out the original and successful poems from among the underbrush of conventionalities in which they lie hidden. It is tempting indeed, in the face of such a mass of material, to react sharply against the triteness of the lesser poems and discard the whole body of the work as not worth the effort. Yet the author of this study is convinced that such a reaction represents a hasty and unjustified rejection of much material of quality. A careful reading discloses the fact that beneath the cloak of conventionality there is to be found in Müller a lyric poet of depth and sensitivity. We are convinced that his works have been unjustly ignored and that it is time to reëvaluate them. In undertaking such a reëvaluation it is necessary to restrict ourselves to a few works of quality. The present study therefore does not present a survey of Müller's entire lyrical production. We have chosen to limit our discussion to three lyric song-cycles. These are the two above-mentioned cycles set to music by Schubert, plus the collection "Frühlingskranz aus dem Plauenschen Grunde bei Dresden," a work unfortunately systematically ignored to the present day. The choice of these three cycles is not arbitrary. It consciously lays aside collections drawn from a limited thematic context ("Griechenlieder," "Johannes und Esther," "Muscheln von der Insel Rügen") and focuses upon the three works which exemplify the lyric quality of Müller's poetry in its purest form. Each of the three cycles represents an artistic unity. Our interpretation of each work will concentrate upon the poems of particular interest. The largely conventional or trite poems will be discussed only briefly or omitted if they do not contribute significantly to the cycle as a whole. This method of interpretation is necessitated by the disparate quality of the poems within each cycle, as discussed above.

In the present study the measure of the quality of a given poem will be seen in the degree to which the poem is successful as a purely lyrical creation. If conventional imagery is employed the poem may be considered successful if this imagery is brought to life by a fresh handling, by the manner in which it is rendered subservient to a spontaneous lyrical statement. This interpretive method will of necessity lead us from various sides into the domain of the poet's creative imagination and will provide the ultimate justification for a reëvaluation. The question that must be answered is whether through a deeper appreciation of his works the poet's unique creative individuality comes alive. We shall address ourselves to this question in a fourth chapter concerned with the unique posture of Müller's poetic imagination—a posture which shows itself to be astonishingly profound for one hitherto considered naïve to the point of superficiality.

By way of introduction to the present study we will give here a brief account of the poet's life. Detailed information will be found in the critical edition of Hatfield and in other works listed in the annotated Bibliography.

Wilhelm Müller was born on October 7, 1794, as the son of a shoemaker in Dessau. At age three, little Wilhelm found himself the only one of the family's seven children that was still alive. His mother died when he was only fourteen. Illness and poverty in the family were counterbalanced by a strong religious feeling and great industry. Müller's alert mind and poetic tendencies asserted themselves even during the school years, when he was known to cover the slate boards with verse.

In 1812, Müller enrolled at the University in Berlin. His studies were interrupted the next year by the political situation, and he volunteered for military service and fought in several engagements. At age twenty-one he returned to the university where he studied philology and history. While in Berlin he fell in love with Luise Hensel, a girl of pious disposition who did not answer Müller's rapturous attention in kind. At this time he and a group of young friends published a volume of patriotic poems entitled *Bundesblüthen* (1816). Müller's interest in the older German literature led to a study of such works as the *Nibelungenlied* and the poetry of the minnesingers. In 1817, Müller began his critical activities with a number of articles published in the *Gesellschafter*, edited by F. W. Gubitz. This was the beginning of a lifelong outpouring of critical works, an activity which literally wore him out.

On August 20, 1817, Müller set out as the travelling companion of Baron Sack on a journey which was to have taken them to Egypt, where Müller was to collect inscriptions for the "Königliche Akademie der Wissenschaften" in Berlin. In Vienna Müller was in contact with many Greek intellectuals. He had recently learned modern Greek, and here the seeds were sown which led to his later fame as the poet of the cause of Greek independence. An outbreak of the plague in Constantinople forced the travellers to proceed to Italy. In Venice Müller experienced the *commedia dell' arte*, and the whole stay in Italy was meaningful to him particularly in terms of his concern with the life and poetry of the common people ("Volk"). Difficulties in Müller's relationship with Baron Sack led to the termination of their plans. The Baron proceeded alone to Egypt, and in 1818 Müller was back in Dessau, where he was forced by a lack of funds to accept a teaching position as "Gehülfslehrer" (1819). He exchanged this activity the following year for a position as librarian.

Müller's literary activities soon assumed very encompassing proportions. He wrote commentaries on a wide variety of literary subjects, including a number of English poets, for the journals of the day. His editorship of the first ten volumes of the *Bibliothek deutscher Dichter des 17. Jahrhunderts* (Brockhaus) represents a distinct contribution to the rediscovery of the then neglected Baroque literature and is a clear example of the intense scholarly activity which complemented Müller's own poetic creation.

In 1821, Müller married Adelheid Basedow, the granddaughter of the famed pedagogue. One of their children, Max Müller, later became a distinguished professor of oriental languages at Oxford. He relates an anecdote which he heard from Rückert in the year 1845, as he was studying Persian under the latter in Berlin. During Müller's stay in Italy he and Rückert had one evening stopped at a poor inn and were plagued by vermin. In an attempt to escape the latter they jumped into the nearby lake. It seems that Rückert could not swim and was on the point of drowning when Wilhelm Müller managed to bring him to shore, saving his life.[4]

Müller's lyrical production kept pace with his scholarly and critical activities. The first larger collection of his poems, volume I of the *Gedichte aus den hinterlassenen Papieren eines reisenden Waldhornisten* appeared in 1820. The second edition of this volume (1826) carries the dedication: "Seinem hoch verehrten und innig geliebten Freunde *Ludwig Tieck* zum Danke für mannigfache Belehrung und Ermunterung gewidmet." Volume II, similarly dedicated to the composer Carl Maria von Weber, appeared in 1824. The "Griechenlieder" were published throughout the years 1821 to 1826.

This period of intense activity was relieved by the proper pastime of a romantic wanderer—travel. Müller undertook a number of longer trips. In 1824, he spent a very happy spring season in beautiful surroundings near Dresden. The result of this visit was the collection of poems entitled "Frühlingskranz aus dem Plauenschen Grunde bei Dresden." In the summer of the following year we find Müller as the guest of the poet Furchau on the island of Rügen in the Baltic. This trip led to the collection "Muscheln von der Insel Rügen." Both of these works, together with the Italian poems, two hundred epigrams, and various other assorted lyrics, appeared in Müller's last major volume, the *Lyrische Reisen und epigrammatische Spaziergänge*. This volume, accompanied by a dedication to Müller's friend Alexander Baron v. Simolin, was published in the year of the poet's death, 1827.

In the hopes of bettering his deteriorating physical condition Müller travelled in Simolin's company to Franzensbrunn bei Eger in Bohemia in July 1826. A letter from Heine, written on the seventh of June of this year, expresses that poet's sense of indebtedness to Müller:

> ... Ich bin groß genug, Ihnen offen zu bekennen, daß mein kleines Intermezzo-Metrum nicht blos zufällige Ähnlichkeit mit Ihrem gewöhnlichen Metrum hat, sondern daß es wahrscheinlich seinen geheimsten Tonfall Ihren Liedern verdankt... Ja, ich bin groß genug, es sogar bestimmt zu wiederholen, und Sie werden es mal öffentlich ausgesprochen finden, daß mir durch die Lecture Ihrer 77 Gedichte zuerst klar geworden, wie man aus den alten, vorhandenen Volksliedformen neue Formen bilden kann, die ebenfalls volksthümlich sind, ohne daß man nöthig hat, die alten Sprachholperigkeiten und Unbeholfenheiten nachzuahmen...
>
> ... Ich bin eitel genug, zu glauben, daß mein Name einst, wenn wir Beide nicht mehr sind, mit dem Ihrigen zusammen genannt wird—darum laßt uns auch im Leben liebevoll verbunden sein.[5]

Despite the intimate tone of the letter, the two poets evidently never met. On the return trip to Dessau Müller passed through Weimar, where he visited Goethe on the latter's seventy-seventh birthday.

The next year the poet was completely exhausted and in precarious health. He decided to undertake a trip with his wife through the Rhineland and Southern Germany. The highlight of this journey was the period spent in Swabia, where Müller met with poets such as Gustav Schwab, Hauff, Uhland and Justinus Kerner. He and Adelheid were everywhere received with the warmest cordiality. In Weinsberg Müller was greeted by a Greek flag which Kerner had made and hoisted atop the stone tower in which Lenau once worked on his *Faust*. Müller seemed pale and failing; in the evening he sat with Kerner and discussed various matters with which Kerner was conversant: death, the life after death, premonitions, spirits, etc. He even persuaded Kerner to take him downstairs to see the latter's famous patient, the "Seherin von Prevorst."[6] On the following morning the Müllers' departure took place under a strange sign. Kerner had been confused as to the colors of the Greek flag and had made a black cross on a blue and white background. The background was subsequently washed away by the rain and fog during the night, and the departing travellers were greeted from Kerner's little tower by a wet white flag with a black cross.

The pair arrived in Weimar on September 19th and remained several days. On the twenty-first they met Goethe, who later commented acidly to Chancellor von Müller: "Es ist mir eine unangenehme Personnage, suffisant, überdies Brillen tragend, was mir das Unleidlichste ist."[7] This sharp reaction may be due partially to Müller's moribund appearance and was doubtless also partially the result of his criticism of Goethe's translations of Greek poetry in *Kunst und Altertum*.[8]

At the end of September Müller felt very happy to be back with his family in Dessau. The evening of the thirtieth he wrote fifteen letters and went early to bed. During the night a heart attack killed him suddenly and painlessly. The documents confirm the fact that death occurred shortly after midnight, so that the poet actually died on the first of October 1827, the first day of the month in which he would have celebrated his thirty-third birthday.

I

Die schöne Müllerin

The final version of the song-cycle "Die schöne Müllerin," published in 1820, consists of twenty-three poems which are framed by a prologue and an epilogue. This frame will not concern us here. The cycle represents the last stage in a long development, the details of which have been described by Bruno Hake.[1] The opera of Paesiello *La Molinaria* (1788), which had appeared on the German stage as *Die schöne Müllerin*, provided the source from which a group of Müller's friends drew the thematic material for a parlor operetta (*Liederspiel*) which they performed in Berlin in 1816-1817, with Müller in the role of the miller's boy. Upon the suggestion of Ludwig Berger, who in 1818 had set ten of the songs (five of them Müller's) to music, Müller undertook to arrange his poems in the form of a song-cycle. This process resulted in the final version, published in 1820 in the collection *Sieben und siebzig Gedichte aus den hinterlassenen Papieren eines reisenden Waldhornisten*. Our present discussion will treat the poems included in this final version, with the exception of the prologue and epilogue.

A large number of themes and images in the work are taken directly from the German folksong tradition.[2] Such items as the mill itself, the lute, or the poetical-allegorical nature of the characters' rustic vocations are stock ingredients of this tradition. Indeed, the hunter who shoots at hearts as well as at game is known even to medieval poetry.[3] Drawing on this tradition, Müller combines his lyric poems into a playlet on the theme of unrequited love. In the prologue he refers to the work as a "monodrama." The dramatic structure proceeds in an ascending line which reaches its climax in the poem "Mein!" After a "pause" ("Pause," "Mit dem grünen Lautenbande") the poem "Der Jäger" introduces the crisis. This is followed by a descending line which preserves the monologue until in the last two poems part of the scenery, the brook itself, speaks.

The cycle contains a number of poems which further the dramatic development, yet are of limited artistic merit. These will be mentioned only when necessary for clarification of the plot or because they contain an image which is significant in the larger context. An image such as that of the window which separates the lover from the girl will recur very frequently in Müller's poetry. Such stock motifs and situations, once identified, are easily spotted by the reader. We shall therefore confine ourselves to tracing the essential elements of the cycle and to interpreting in detail those poems which are unusually successful. The uniqueness of Müller's creative talent reveals itself in the manner in which he employs the conventional material, recasting it in his own mold. The nature of his personal lyrical ability will reveal itself as we examine the specific poems of particular interest.[4]

In the opening poem, "Wanderschaft," (p. 118) the archetypal romantic theme of wandering sets the tone for the entire cycle. The double refrain in each stanza gives rhythmical expression to the revolving of the millwheel.

The first stanza connects the theme of *Wanderlust* with the miller's vocation. The reason for the miller's sensitivity to the temptations of wandering is expressed in stanza two: "Vom Wasser haben wir's gelernt." In water, as the element which never rests, nature provides an example of wandering. The motif, attached in the third stanza to the turning wheels, is heightened in the fourth. Here nature's most permanent and immobile element, stone, is itself set into motion as the millstones grind the grain. They "dance" and wish to go even faster. This quaint image is characteristic of the urge of romanticism to animate all of creation—to set the entire universe in motion, for the word "Steine" suggests not only the millstones but also "das Gestein"—the very rock under our feet.

In the fifth stanza the change from third to first person address creates an entirely *inner* perspective: "O Wandern, Wandern meine Lust." Through the fusion of the poet's own being with that of the role of the miller's boy in the lyrical "I," the motif of *Wandern* functions as a primary moving force within the soul of the poet himself.

The refrain, carrier of the underlying revolving rhythm, is not frozen in mechanical repetition but is actually transformed in each stanza ("das Wandern ... das Wasser ... die Räder" etc.), imparting a forward stride to the movement. This aspect is enhanced by the placement of the refrain within the stanza itself, for it always appears after first *one* and then after *two* lines. In this way the poet avoids any danger of monotony and enlivens the poem with a forward-flowing rhythm. Such a detail as this, which seems so very natural once it is recognized, provides a clear example of Wilhelm Müller's unusually keen musical sensitivity.

Through the repetition of the word "Lust" at the end, a bridge is established to the first stanza, and a poem which otherwise might be in danger of – literally – overflowing its bounds, is rounded out as a unified statement. As we shall observe in the course of our study, this odd combination of freely flowing musicality and architectural stability of form is a cornerstone of the workings of Wilhelm Müller's poetic imagination.

The poem "Wohin?" (p. 119) picks up the image of flowing water, beginning with the lines "Ich hört' ein Bächlein rauschen / Wohl aus dem Felsenquell," lines directly inspired by the German folksong tradition. Bretano's "Ich hör' ein Sichlein rauschen / Wohl rauschen durch das Korn" and similar passages are to be found in this tradition, which encompasses *Des Knaben Wunderhorn* as well as other sources.[5] The first two lines of the last stanza are similarly patterned after the folksong, as is also the line "Ich weiß nicht, wie mir wurde" (stanza two, line one), which appears there in the present tense. Such borrowings are found throughout Müller's poetry. We must now look at the way in which he incorporates them into his own poem.

The first impression of the poem is acoustical, and as such transmits a sense of the scene which is more diffused, less plastic than a visual impression would be. Through the word "wunderhell" an atmosphere of enchantment is conjured up, which in the course of the poem will increase in intensity. The locale "Wohl aus dem Felsenquell" is also indefinite and mysterious. We sense only an impression of rushing water pouring down from above and experience it solely in the acoustical sphere.

The poet himself is unable to describe his impression (stanza two: "Ich weiß nicht, wie mir wurde"). The psychological reaction is irrational, and it is compelling: "Ich mußte gleich hinunter / Mit meinem Wanderstab." With the introduction of the walking stick the motif of *Wanderlust*, subject of the first poem, is united with the acoustical experience which in this second poem exercises an undefined psychological power over the wanderer's inner life. The miller's boy no longer feels merely a *desire* to wander (*Wander-Lust*)—he feels inwardly impelled. It should again be noted that while these poems are spoken through the role of the miller's boy, this role represents merely the outward costume, the vehicle employed by the author to clothe his thoughts. We must not fall into the error of viewing poems of such conventional and stylized origin as *Bekenntnislyrik* in the Goethean sense. Yet in the face of a treatment which is often profound in content and subtle in form we shall wish to uncover the level of experience which lies beneath the conventionality and evidences the poet's own inner world. An interpretation which arbitrarily separates the two realms in an absolute sense closes its eyes to the mode of expression of the "lyrical I," which unites within it the world of experience without (including the "I" of the role in question) and that within the poet's own being. It is therefore our hope that this methodological aside will assure the reader that in speaking now of "the miller's boy" and now of "the poet" we are doing so in full consciousness of the lyrical posture involved. The reader is referred to the discussion of Müller's song-cycles in the recent helpful article by Klaus Günther Just,[6] who carefully analyzes the workings and compass of the "lyrical I" in these poems.

The third stanza picks up the word "hinunter" from stanza two and through a series of repetitions ("Und immer ...") unites the auditory and visual impressions in a rushing, hypnotic rhythm that sweeps the poet along.[7]

An important point in the cycle is reached in the fourth stanza with the poet's reaction to the experience: "Ist das denn meine Straße?" The lyrical "I" senses an inner involvement with the onward rush of the water and therefore directs this highly personal question to the brook. The intimate relation between brook and "I", which will become clearly manifest when in the last two poems the personified stream begins to speak, is now brought to light through the poet's question. The brook represents imaginatively a higher guiding force, a stream of destiny which accompanies man through life. Because this force of destiny, leading man from one experience to the next, is largely inscrutable (as its metaphor, the water, is transparent), only an inkling of its workings is present and calls forth the question.[8]

The last two lines of stanza four strengthen the impression of magic intoxication alluded to already in the first stanza ("wunderhell"). The "Rauschen" of the water without wells up into a "Berauschung" of emotion within, until in stanza five this sound-magic is metamorphosed into the voices of a sphere of watersprites behind the acoustical impressions: "Es singen wohl die Nixen / Dort unten ihren Reihn." Here the high point (or more properly, the low point) in the poem is reached, as the poet's consciousness is flooded by the sweet singing of elemental beings over which he has no control. The motif "Wandern-Müssen" is thus heightened into the sphere of enchantment. The whole experience is then accepted in the last stanza, and the poet willingly follows the course in which the brook leads him. He senses the inner guiding force of his destiny ("meine Straße") and accepts the stream's leadership in the confidence that he will "find his way" ("Es gehn ja Mühlenräder / In jedem klaren Bach"). The simple little poem contains, in metaphorical distillation, a picture of a deep mystery of human life. Its title "Wohin?" is a question directed to the stream of destiny.

In the next three poems ("Halt," "Danksagung an den Bach," "Am Feierabend," (pp. 119-121) the magic intoxication within the miller boy's soul is overcome by the concrete encounter with the world of the mill and the miller's daughter.[9] Characteristic of this change is the shift in the acoustical perceptions. The roar of water and attendant singing of the nixies is literally broken through by the very "realistic" mechanical rattling of the millwheel: "Durch Rauschen und Singen / Bricht Rädergebraus." The cheerful and homey atmosphere is enhanced by the mention of the girl's window, an image which occurs repeatedly in Müller's poetry.[10] This motif is rich in expressive potential through the polarity of its metaphorical compass. The window is an opening which enables the lovers to see one another, while at the same time maintaining an invisible barrier which separates the two.

The poem "Am Feierabend" (p. 120) gives vent to the boy's youthful joy and presents an idyllic evening scene in the miller's home. The tension between the foregoing passionately expressed personal sentiments and the present portrayal of the miller's daughter wishing *all* a good night lays the foundation for the conflict to come. We sense that the lad's idealization of the girl may be leading him into illusory hopes regarding her feelings.[11] Thus the ultimate tragedy is subtly prepared early in the cycle by such details as the image of the brook rushing downwards into the valley and the present portrayal of a young heart cherishing hopes not really justified by the realities of the situation.

The next two poems ("Der Neugierige," "Das Mühlenleben," pp. 121-122) present once again the complementary poles of introspective searching (questions put to the stream) and outward commentary upon the life situation in which the boy finds himself. The introduction of the images of flowers and stars, symbols of the earthly and heavenly spheres, prepares the way for their deepened treatment in the poem "Thränenregen."[12] Nature provides no answer to the lad's query, and he again turns to the brook, that he feels may assure him of the girl's love. Schubert's treatment of the central stanza of "Der Neugierige" is of the greatest poignancy, and rightly so. For the key word is "stumm." The intimate charm of the poem lies in the almost audible *silence* which greets the boy's sincere questionings. The manner in which the question is formulated is eminently characteristic of Müller's poetic imagination. It is conceived in the form of a strict polarity—the answer must be either "Ja" or "Nein," for this polarity encompasses all possibilities of happiness or unhappiness: "Die beiden Wörtchen schließen / Die ganze Welt mir ein." At the core of this poem (stanza three), the delicate searching for an answer from the silent stream twice calls forth the numeral "ein," the second italicized by Müller: "Will ja nur Eines wissen, / *Ein* Wörtchen um und um." Curiously enough, this little word will now slip under the surface of the narrative and come forth again as the resounding refrain which echoes through the poem "Mein," the poem which presents the boy's overflowing conviction that the question he has asked truly *has* been answered.

The poem "Ungeduld" (p. 123), a perennial favorite in the Schubert *Lieder* repertoire, represents a refinement and transformation of the message of "Am Feierabend." The one central sentiment of love, carried by the refrain "Dein ist mein Herz, und soll es ewig bleiben," is elaborated through the enumeration of various vehicles for its expression: bark, stones, bird, wind, etc.[13] Not until the next to the last line of the poem does reality reassert itself: "Und sie merkt nichts von all' dem bangen Treiben." The poem is almost entirely cast in the subjunctive mood. Only two positive statements in the indicative are to be found. These are the abovementioned line and the refrain itself, which is also only a positive assertion of the boy's wish. Thus the next to the last line stands in vivid contrast to the rest of the poem. The miller's daughter notices nothing unusual in the same world of nature which from the lad's point of view ought to ("müßt'") exhaust its active life in the expression of his love. It is for this reason that the poem, despite its passionate tone, is at bottom so very delicate. All is held in the tenuous sphere of *hope*, and the one reflection which is expressed in the indicative assures us (and the poet as well) that it will remain in this sphere. This striking contrast is reflected on another level in the happy choice of words in the key line. The word "Treiben," which carries the forward thrust of the boy's wishes, is modified by the adjective "bang," which gives expression to his apprehension. In this tense juxtaposition "banges Treiben" we have in a sense the whole message of the poem *in nuce*. Similarly, the central psychological problem of the cycle itself is contained within this poem *in nuce*. Although he secretly senses that his love will go unanswered, the young man passionately attempts to marshal all of natural creation in the service of this love. But the girl hears—nothing.

"Thränenregen" (p. 125) provides a clear example of Müller's ability to breathe life into conventional material.[14] On the surface the images are thoroughly traditional, yet the poem is of considerable interest. Its iambic-anapestic rhythm imitates the rippling of the stream. But also the content is here particularly deserving of closer scrutiny. It may be viewed on two levels. First, the poem presents an intensified treatment of the basic psychological conflict between the miller boy's illusory hopes and the real fact of the girl's indifference to them. The intensification inheres in the fact that the two are here brought into intimate physical proximity, yet are abruptly separated by a caprice of nature: "... Es kommt ein Regen, / Ade, ich geh' nach Haus." Secondly, the poem may be viewed with reference to the deeper question of the boy's inner searchings, of his "way through life" as these express themselves throughout the cycle in the metaphorical treatment of flowing water.

The mood of the first stanza is one of intimacy ("traulich"). Yet despite the fact that for the first time in the cycle the two are portrayed in close physical proximity, no dialogue arises. The feeling of unbridgeable distance which the reader, conditioned by the previous poems, clearly senses, is confirmed by the end of the poem. In stanza two the scene is greatly expanded as the coming of night is described through the appearance of moon and stars. The introduction of the motif of the mirror, as this is created by the surface of the water, provides the context whereby the illusory quality of the love relationship can be handled in the most organic way. K. G. Just points to the important fact that the boy's subsequent confusion of stars and flowers with the girl's eyes upsets the latter's stable position as points of reference ("Fixpunkte") for the lover.[15] The "heaven" he is so anxiously seeking to find in the person of the miller's daughter reveals itself to him only in reflected form and as such must remain unattainable.

The whole picture is deepened when we look closely at the manner in which the heavenly bodies are introduced: "Und schauten so traulich zusammen / In den silbernen Spiegel hinein." The conscious repetition of the figure "... schauten so traulich zusammen," associated in the first stanza with the two young people, subtly unites the sphere of these personified heavenly bodies and the activities of man. Through the musicality of the stanzas (repetition, metre) and this alignment of imagery we experience a delicate interweaving of the cosmos and the human sphere. It is no accident that this mysterious interaction takes place through the medium of *water*, the element which in this song-cycle is metaphorically associated with the sphere of invisible forces which form destiny—i.e., connect man with a higher order of things, as this sphere finds artistic expression in the image of the stream. We are now touching upon a very deep dimension of the cycle's poetic content, which will reveal its underlying meaning more clearly in the last poems.

The ultimate impossibility of the love relationship hoped for by the boy is woven into the first two stanzas in the subtlest possible form. As we have noted, the magical coming-together of imagery is carried by such devices as repetition ("traulich ... traulich"). This device governs the choice of rhyme of lines one and three of each of these stanzas. In stanza one the rhyme is "beisammen ... zusammen." In stanza two, the stanza in which the image of the *mirror* and its associations of reflection and illusion occurs, the rhyme—interestingly enough—falls apart: "gekommen ... zusammen." There is an almost uncanny appropriateness in this seemingly unfortunate little discrepancy in the rhyme scheme.

The boy looks down into the brook (now endowed with the epithet "selig") into the reflected eyes of the girl. The introduction of a heavily anapestic rhythm in stanza four provides the natural musical undercurrent for the expansion of the reflection to include the little blue flowers, which, like a host of tiny blue eyes, dance and bob about on the wavelets ("Sie nickten und blickten ihr nach").

Whereas in stanza four the mirror surface of the water is broken, allowing the girl's eyes and the flowers to gaze upwards at the boy, the fifth stanza brings a complete metamorphosis of the vision: "Und in den Bach versunken / Der ganze Himmel schien." The very cosmos itself is now magically contained within the watery element. We need only remind ourselves of the identification of this brook with the workings of destiny in the life of the boy to realize the sheer scope and grandeur of spiritual suggestiveness woven into this ephemeral vision. Its full implications will be seen at the end of the cycle.

The present moment can only be fleeting. The gaze into a magical world of reflected images wrenches the boy's consciousness out of its proper relationship to the solid ground under him, and the dangerous forces of enchantment already associated with the water in "Wohin?" again assert themselves, this time attached to the reflection of the stars: "Und wollte mich mit hinunter / In seine Tiefe ziehn," a first indirect hint at the suicide by drowning to which the lad will succumb in the end. Most appropriate is the use of the possessive adjective "seine" in the above passage, for this grammatical form refers both to the brook ("der Bach") and to the heavens ("der Himmel"). Even through their embodiment in the realm of grammar the starry ocean and the water of the stream are completely united.

In the sixth stanza the cosmic-earthly vision is further transformed and deepened, while the theme of enchantment and temptation is intensified:

> Und über den Wolken und Sternen
> Da rieselte munter der Bach,
> Und rief mit Singen und Klingen:
> Geselle, Geselle, mir nach!

The normal vertical spatial coordinates are now entirely reversed as the brook rushes along *over* the stars and moon which it has entirely incorporated within itself. At this point at which the phenomena of nature and with them the boy's consciousness are virtually turned inside-out the formula "Singen und Klingen" appears as a direct echo from "Danksagung an den Bach." The enticing nixie-music ("Wohin?") again becomes audible. Müller's keen musical sense gives it embodiment through the device of repetition ("Geselle, Geselle, mir nach!") imparting to the entire stanza an enticing, hypnotic gesture.

With the coming of a sudden shower in stanza six the raindrops obliterate the images reflected in the water's surface, the vision is erased, and the boy is swiftly propelled back into the prosaic world of everyday reality. Curiously it is the water itself which erases the magic vision held in the water of the brook. Through an unexpected whim the natural element undoes its own magical workings. The emotional disappointment of the boy in the face of the girl's disinterest has been the object of the siren-like singing from under the waves and now breaks forth in the conventional image of flowing tears. Just as in "Ungeduld" the next to the last line ("Und sie merkt nichts von all' dem bangen Treiben") cuts through the boy's wishful daydreams, so too does the girl's exclamation "Es kommt ein Regen, / Ade, ich geh' nach Haus" jolt the reader back to the everyday situation. The rising dramatic pitch of the cycle's construction is evident in the difference between these two poems. In "Ungeduld" the girl is not present and the key line mentioned is spoken by the boy *about* her. In "Thränenregen" the two are brought together and the key line which reintroduces everyday reality is actually spoken by the girl. The fact that these trivial words are the only ones spoken in the poem, despite the assurances that the encounter was very "traulich," enhances the tragic-ironic tone.

At its deepest metaphorical level this poem enlarges the role of the stream as bearer of destiny through presenting the water itself as symbolic of a sphere in which outer nature (in the largest sense the cosmos) and the inner, spiritual world of man are united. The experience presents itself as a flowing world of imaginative pictures. A similar treatment is found in the collection of poems published in the year 1826 under the title "Muscheln von der Insel Rügen."[16] In the introductory poem of this collection, entitled "Muscheln," Müller speaks of the muse that wanders along the sea shore collecting mussels: "Dann schweift die Mus' umher am nassen Strande / und sammelt kleine Muscheln sich zu Kränzen." The mussels are metaphors for the poems gathered up by the muse into wreaths,—i.e., into collections (cf. "Frühlings*kranz*"). The mussels are children of the ocean, born beneath the waves and cast up onto the shore. The meaning is clear: the inner, spiritual world of flowing pictures and musicality out of which the poet draws his inspirations is seen metaphorically in the flooding tides of the ocean. The world of Müller's poetic imagination is inwardly consistent, and it is rather profound. The poet knew that in entering into such an imaginative sphere one exposes oneself not only to experiences of great, even cosmic beauty ("der *selige* Bach," moon, stars) but also to certain temptations and a lack of stability ("Geselle, Geselle, mir nach!"). In the present poem nature itself steps in at the critical juncture. Just as the boy loses control of his emotions and bursts into tears, the summer shower sweeps by, and breaks the dangerous spell.

In the poem "Mein" (p. 125) the refrain of "Ungeduld," "Dein ist mein Herz, und soll es ewig bleiben" has contracted into the one little word "Mein!" which echoes through all of nature as a joyful message of love. Not only through its distillation of the love-message but also through its structure and placement this poem represents the apex of the dramatic line of the entire cycle.

All of the freely flowing trochaic lines rhyme on the syllable *-ein*. This syllable also appears in the form of the indefinite article as the central word in the central line of the poem, where it is even italicized: "Schalle heut' *ein* Reim allein." Through its position at dead center it forms an axis around which the entire poem revolves. Yet this is not all. This mathematically accurate placement of the rhyme-word in the exact center of the central line of the poem corresponds precisely to the placement of the poem itself in the structure of the entire cycle. As the twelfth among twenty-three poems it occupies the exact middle position. Eleven poems precede and eleven follow it.

From the standpoint of content as well as form this poem is unique. Through the overwhelming, though illusory belief in the fulfillment of love, the dramatic pinnacle of the cycle is reached. The action has risen (poems 1-11), strikes here its highest point (poem 12) and falls gradually off to the tragic end (poems 13-23). The "monodrama's" unity ("Ein-heit"!) could not have found more fitting expression than through the mathematically precise central placement of the rhyme syllable "ein" in the cycle.

The poet, having built up to the ecstatic avowal of his love ("Die geliebte Müllerin ist *mein*! / *Mein*!"), turns to nature, from which he hopes to elicit a heightening of her beauties which as a sympathetic reaction will verify his emotional state. When such a reaction is not forthcoming he once again finds himself isolated. This emotional disillusionment which thematically anticipates the tragic outcome of the cycle is a heightening of the experience portrayed in "Ungeduld" and "Thränenregen." The dramatic thrust is however greatly increased through the totality of the poet's claims. Both the inner and the outer worlds are here intensified to the level of absolutes—the inner through complete ego-saturation ("... *mein*! / *Mein*!"), the outer through the expansion of the natural environment to include all of creation ("Unverstanden in der weiten Schöpfung...").

In "Der Neugierige" (p. 121) the poet had implored the stream to speak the one word, yes or no, which would put his heart at rest: "Will ja nur Eines wissen, / Ein Wörtchen um und um"). The scope ("Ja" or "Nein") and uncompromising intensity of that question clearly pointed to its central thematic importance for the outcome of the monodrama. It is therefore only logical that the answer to the question, the "one little word" ("Mein!"), should break forth in the central poem of the cycle and that the italicized indefinite article "*ein*" of the question ("*Ein* Wörtchen um und um") should reappear, italicized, in the poem which brings the answer—indeed, that it should appear there as the central word of the poem ("Schalle heut' *ein* Reim allein"). Through such subtle links as this the cycle is organically knit together.

The complementary functions of content and form in this poem point to an inherent statement concerning the function of poetry itself. The frustration of the boy's desired union with the girl through love results in his continued sense of isolation. This mood finds expression in the unbridgeable chasm between himself and nature, between "I" and world. We have seen, however, that the longing for unity which is incapable of fulfillment in nature is brought about *in the poem* through the functioning of form. The "Ein-heit" sought in vain in the outer world is accomplished by the poet in the aesthetic sphere. The message of love which is not understood in the world ("Unverstanden in der weiten Schöpfung") is given tragically sweet permanency in the realm of art. For the message of love is a message which speaks of a uniting ("Ver-ein-igung"), a uniting which may be unattainable in the everyday world but may on rare occasions be conjured forth by a sensitive poet through the magical musicality of language, as an "Ein-heit" beyond intellectual analysis.

The dramatic structure of the cycle is again underscored by the placement of the poem "Pause" (p. 126). The action has reached its height in "Mein," and the present poem provides an hiatus before the motion gradually descends.[17] The function of the poem is carried by its formal handling. The long, four and five beat lines can only be read slowly, whereby the forward rush of the previous poem is checked. Thematically the puzzled mood of questioning finds clear expression in the last two lines, which inquire whether the sighing tone produced by the ribbon striking the lute strings is a last echo of past emotions or the herald of feelings to come.

The poem's central image, the lute, is taken from the properties box of conventional trappings employed in the knightly romances popular at the time.[18] In the present poem the hanging-up of this instrument represents by an outward gesture the singer's inward state. An excess of emotion forces him to lay aside his song, just as in "Thränenregen" the surge of emotion led to the welling up of tears. In both cases the miller's boy yields under the pressure of uncontrolled sentiments.

The interesting aspect of the theme developed in "Pause" is its reference to the question of the process of poetic creativity, which can develop in a healthy manner only as long as the poet maintains his inner balance. If the balance is upset by inner turmoil the instrument whereby poetry may be expressed remains—literally—hanging. As such it is played upon no longer by a conscious individual but by the whim of nature— the wind, a bee, the dangling ribbon. The result is a formless, eerie music that arises quite independently of the artist's conscious will ("seufzender Klang"). The poet senses clearly the danger inherent in such an abdication of his responsibility: "Da wird mir bange und es durchschauert mich." Once again Müller's handling of this situation is accurate even into the grammar, for the use of the dative and accusative personal pronouns rather forcefully enhances the notion that the poet is here being acted *upon*: "Da wird *mir* bange und es durchschauert *mich*." The central message of the poem is one which is of considerable importance to the question we shall come back to frequently with reference to Wilhelm Müller's poetic imagination—the question as to the nature of the creative process. For Müller the process must remain fully conscious in order to be fruitful. The singer who allows himself to be upset by swells of emotion can only lay aside his lute.

"Mit dem grünen Lautenbande" (p. 126) introduces conventional color associations which featured in the original "Liederspiel." In the folk-tradition the girl was often referred to as "Rose" or "Röschen," and because in nature this flower is surrounded by green foliage she feels drawn toward the hunter, who is associated with green, while the miller's boy is of course recognized by his white appearance.[19]

The lute's green ribbon, linked to the theme of poetry, is now sent to the girl and thereby serves as a motif which unites a number of the themes developed thus far in the cycle: love, hope, music, poetry. Müller also introduces the girl's statement, "Ich hab' das Grün so gern!" which he then transforms, modulating this theme five times in the course of this poem (lines three and six of each stanza). The theme will now disappear and be reintroduced, colored by the irony of the approaching tragedy, in "Die liebe Farbe."

With the entrance of the hunter ("Der Jäger," p. 127) an outer threat is introduced which complements the inner, psychological threat which has been developed in the course of the cycle. The dramatic line is hereby given a vigorous downward turn.[20] The helplessness of the boy in the face of the hunter's appearance is rendered particularly forceful by the expansion of the color symbolism underlying the events. The traditional color of the hunter is of course green, of which the girl has said in the last poem "Ich hab' das Grün so gern!" The themes associated with the color green are thus expanded to include the irreconcilable opposites implied in the miller boy's hope and the objective threat posed by the hunter. The reader clearly senses that the power of the color symbolism is such that the girl and the hunter will be drawn together as by a chromatic *Wahlverwandtschaft*.[21]

The traditional associative use of color is rendered more deeply symbolical in the poems "Die liebe Farbe" and "Die böse Farbe" (pp. 129-130). The theme of death, gently hinted at earlier in the cycle in the temptations of the water spirits, is presented in stark clarity in "Die liebe Farbe." The form of the poem is complicated. It consists of three six-line iambic stanzas, each carrying the following arrangement of accented syllables: 3 3 3 4 4 3. The first two lines end with an unaccented syllable, whereas the following four are accented. The rhyme scheme does not simply follow this pattern however, for it runs *a a b c c b*. These "patterned irregularities" in the poem's formal structure preclude any danger of monotony by maintaining a delicate musicality. The refrain is a direct variation of the theme struck in "Mit dem grünen Lautenbande."

The most interesting feature of this poem is the powerful heightening (*Steigerung*) of the use of the color symbolism. The color green, imbued already with polar associations of hope and impending disaster, is now employed as the background color for the theme of death. The poet desires none of the traditional religious symbols (cross, flowers) but rather a grave enveloped entirely in green.[22] Indeed, the whole picture of death is here presented in a green mantle. The result of this treatment is that the quality of the color is lifted out of the polarity of good and evil and transformed into the medium which leads the way into eternity. Thus the paradox implied in the tension between the color's *positive* (title, refrain) and *negative* (hunter) use is overcome and leads to a higher unity which is possible only in death. The breadth and depth of Müller's employment of the color symbolism in this poem is striking.

The juxtaposition of the titles "Die liebe Farbe" and "Die böse Farbe" also gives expression to the polar associations of the color green. However, this polarity is fully developed in the two poems "Erster Schmerz, letzter Scherz" and "Die liebe Farbe" and even overcome in the second. Therefore, nothing new is added to the metaphorical use of green in "Die böse Farbe." Its function is to gather together the well-known imagery under the theme of leave-taking.[23] The green ribbon is returned, and the handshake represents the formal separation. With the return of the love token the cycle's dramatic structure moves significantly closer to the disastrous conclusion. It is therefore of particular interest to note that it is in this poem that we find specific motifs which form the very substance of the cycle "Die Winterreise." The theme of leave-taking lies at the heart of that cycle. Similarly, the monotonous repetition of words or themes ("Ich möchte," "Ade") is there employed as a conscious technique for the enhancement of the mood of desperation. But most obvious is the introduction in stanza four of the stormy winter landscape: "Ich möchte liegen vor ihrer Thür, / In Sturm und Regen und Schnee." This is anticipated in stanza two, in which the emotion of despair is directed by the boy at the color symbolism itself. This effects a metamorphosis from the green of the foregoing poems to the death-color *par excellence*, white: "Ich möchte die grünen Gräser all' / Weinen ganz todtenbleich." With this clear identification of the miller's color, white, with the sphere of winter, snow and death, the reader senses that the color alchemy of the cycle has now drawn up the lines of the further action quite clearly, and has clamped a seal on the boy's fate.

The remaining four poems form a unit in that they develop the theme of resignation and death, just as the cycle's four introductory poems embodied the mood of hope and confidence in life. The theme of death now casts its shadow even upon the flowers, which wither under the spell of growing despair and form the backdrop for the suicide wish. The image of the cynically-named black "Blümlein Vergißmein" ("Blümlein Vergißmein," p. 130) which grows in a murky garden full of *fleurs de mal*, serves as a vehicle for the theme of a magic curse.[24] The boy now feels *compelled* to follow the path into self-destruction: "Das Blümlein muß ich suchen, / Wie auch die Straße geht." Once again we hear an echo from the beginning of the cycle: "Ist das denn meine Straße? / O Bächlein, sprich, wohin?" ("Wohin?"). The young man no longer is able to ask questions as to which is the right path. The open-minded stance of questioning is replaced by the unswerving intent to self-destruction ("Das Blümlein *muß* ich suchen ...").

Without the slightest hint of the weirdly demonic atmosphere of the poem immediately preceding it, the following poem "Trockne Blumen" (p. 131) celebrates the death and resurrection of the poet's love. The flowers mirror the inward world of dying and reawakening love. Through the concise folksong stanza a naïve simplicity of emotion is maintained. When the girl passes the miller lad's grave and acknowledges the true love he bore to her ("*Der* meint' es treu") the flowers sprout forth as harbingers of spring and tokens of resurrected love.[25]

This poem is of particular interest in that through the boy's wish, which it expresses, it points to a future reawakening which lies beyond the end of the cycle itself. It is also of significance because through this conception of love reawakening at the coming of spring the dilemma of "Die Winterreise" is in a sense already overcome here in the "Müllerin" cycle. The world of "Die Winterreise" has been introduced in "Die böse Farbe," and its icy bleakness is here inwardly conquered by the anticipation of the blossoming of spring, the world of the cycle "Frühlingskranz." We do not wish to imply that "Die Winterreise" is therefore to be viewed as a less valid artistic statement. On the contrary, its very convincing ring is all the more surprising when one realizes that while it was published in 1822 (and likely written during the year 1821) its thematics are anticipated and inwardly transcended in the poem "Trockne Blumen," which belongs to the earliest poems of "Die schöne Müllerin" (1816).

The final two poems in the cycle introduce the stream as an active speaker. In its formal structure "Der Müller und der Bach" (p. 132) functions as a transition from the foregoing monologue of the miller's boy to the last poem of the cycle, a monologue of the stream. The poem includes a collection of *topoi* taken from traditional sources.[26] By painting a picture of the heavenly joy resulting from man's transformed pain the brook attempts to dissuade the boy from drowning himself. The attempt is fruitless, for the young man's anguish is too pressing. In the final stanza the cool peace of death in the water is conceived of in terms of a complete letting-go. The rocking motion, enhanced by the repetition of the vowel *u*, creates a mood of pure musicality. In a sense the death here portrayed may be described on another level as a dissolving of the individuality into a flood of music:

> Ach, unten, da unten,
> Die kühle Ruh'!
> Ach Bächlein, liebes Bächlein,
> So singe nur zu.

We may ask why it is that just at this point a *conversation* arises. Since the beginning of the cycle, the poet has spoken to the brook, to the rushing water in which he senses the presence of a force guiding his destiny. But in his mood of cheerful self-confidence he has sensed this presence only dimly. Only through a psychological shock, however, is the more delicate organ of perception, the lad's "inner" ear, opened. The shock is given through his insight into the hopelessness of his situation (as portrayed, for instance, in "Blümlein Vergißmein"). The magnitude of the shock is understandable when the youthful naïveté of the boy is taken into consideration. His total claim to love, when frustrated, yields to total despair. Only at the edge of the abyss is the lad so shaken that his entire attention shifts from the outer world and focuses upon his own inner state. Once this has happened there is born within him a new inner *hearing* which perceives the voice of his "stream" (one might call it his higher spiritual self) no longer as dim music, but as spoken *word* within the soul. Not until this point has been reached does a true *conversation* develop. It is rather a deep insight which lies behind this shift from monologue to dialogue within the cycle's formal structure.

The final poem, "Des Baches Wiegenlied" (p. 133), is outstanding and must be interpreted in detail. This lullaby, sung by the stream after the miller's lad has cast himself into the water, breaks through the conventional scenery with a vision of sublime peace. The irregularity of unstressed syllables in the basically iambic lines loosens the metrical pattern and suggests the soft undulation of the waves.

The title points to the central experience of the poem—the boy is lulled by the brook into the sleep of death. The *u* from the last line of the preceding poem ("so singe nur zu") is carried over into the first line of this one ("Gute Ruh', gute

Ruh'!"). Strengthened by repetition within the line itself it weaves an undercurrent of pure musicality for the unfolding cradle-song. The boy is rocked to sleep in the arms of the stream whose consciousness is eternal as well as temporal and who is thus able to speak of the world beyond death. The ever recurrent motif of *wandering* finds its goal in the sea of eternity: "Wandrer, du müder, du bist zu Haus." Similarly, the theme of fidelity (*Treue*) finds its fulfillment in this realm in which all individual destinies are gathered up into eternity: "Bis das Meer will trinken die Bächlein aus."

A beautiful transformation of the world of the elemental spirits which dwell in the water is portrayed in stanza two. The boy is bedded down in his watery grave, and a scene of delicate enchantment lights up before our eyes: "In dem blauen krystallenen Kämmerlein." This color, which carries associations of flowers (forget-me-not), the loved one's eyes, and heavenly feelings in general, now envelops the boy, who is described in stanza five as asleep. One is reminded of the crystal casket in which Snow White lies enchanted until the day of her reanimation (stanza five: "Gute Nacht, gute Nacht! / Bis Alles wacht ...").

The brook now addresses its own watery element, which, as we know, is the home of the nixies and elemental spirits ("Wohin?," stanza five). These spirits are now conjured forth upon the waves of repetition: "Heran, heran, / Was wiegen kann," which is strengthened by the alliteration: "Woget und wieget den Knaben mir ein!" This world of the nixies which had sought to cast a charm of temptation upon the lad in the rushing roar of the water has now transformed itself into the wonderfully clear, blue chamber ("krystallene[s] Kämmerlein"). The change is apparent even in the use of sound, for the alliterating *k* expresses a quality diametrically opposed to the otherwise amorphous watery element. It embodies the hard, angular quality of the crystal through whose edges and corners the blue light is reflected.

The brook seeks to protect the sleeper from all the disturbing elements, such as the huntsman's horn, the blue flowers, and the shadow of the girl herself.[27]

In stanza five the brook sings its lullaby in a gently rocking rhythm: "Gute Nacht, gute Nacht! / Bis Alles wacht." The religiosity of the entire context thus comes into focus as the theme of death is linked to that of an awakening to a higher life. This clarifies the meaning of the poem's title, which speaks of a lullaby. The boy's tragic death is thereby imbued with suggestions of new birth through the image of the child in the cradle.

The entire spectrum of emotions is now to be laid aside in the realm of eternity: "Schlaf' aus deine Freude, schlaf' aus dein Leid!" Once again we find that Müller conceives of such a phenomenon in terms of a *polarity* which is denoted by a cliché-like formula ("Freud / Leid"). We will find such formulae throughout Müller's poetry. In "Der Neugierige" the answer to the key question is to be either "Ja" or "Nein"; and in the second stanza of the famous "Der Lindenbaum" we find the formula "in Freud' und Leide." A deeper investigation of Müller's poetic imagination reveals the fact that such formulae occur so frequently for the simple reason that they correspond to a central feature of his inner nature. He did not by any means experience reality merely in terms of a flood of rather unstructured romantic emotionalism. On the contrary, the most cursory investigation of his critical writings and a reading of his witty and intellectually acute epigrams[28] point to quite the opposite stance. In these there is evidenced a tendency to analyse and measure, to weigh and balance his perceptions architecturally, which leads Müller frequently to view even such qualitative experiences as color in terms of a polarity. This is the deeper explanation of the recurrence of such turns of phrase as "Freud' und Leid" in his lyrical productions.[29] In such a line as the present one ("Schlaf' aus deine Freude, schlaf' aus dein Leid!") the context itself points to a higher synthesis of these opposites in a sphere beyond time and space.

We recall that in "Thränenregen" the moon and stars were reflected in the stream and finally sank deeply into the water, where they were woven together with the reflected flowers and eyes:

> Und in den Bach versunken
> Der ganze Himmel schien,
> Und wollte mich mit hinunter
> In seine Tiefe ziehn.

We spoke in this connection of the delicate interweaving of the worlds of the cosmos and the destiny of man (stars, moon and stream) as touched on by this extraordinary image. We now find a most wonderful metamorphosis of this picture in the last stanza of the cycle. Here it is the stream itself which sings a melodious song describing the moonrise:

> Der Vollmond steigt,
> Der Nebel weicht,
> Und der Himmel da oben, wie ist er so weit!

These lines contain more than a superficial reading would suggest, and we shall therefore examine them in detail.

The progression from the finite to the infinite is here carried both by the imagery and by the language itself. The clearly defined, finite sphere (the moon) slowly and majestically rises. The mist—i.e., all that is cloudy and opaque, gives way ("weicht") before this monumental phenomenon. The word "weicht" implies a victorious power emanating from the rising moon itself, before which the fogs can no longer maintain their positions and are obliged to yield. The classical simplicity of the description conveys a feeling of deep, crystalline clarity.

It is interesting to note that the last line begins with a noun and ends with an adjective. The fixed concept "der Himmel" is thereby gradually dissolved into the non-specific, limitless *quality* inherent in the predicate adjective "weit." Whatever boundaries our consciousness may be accustomed to associate with the sky (or with heaven, as you will) by having been educated to experience the idea in the conceptual straight-jacket it wears when appearing in language as an "it" (i.e., in the form of a "subtantive") are here transcended by the final adjective, which allows our feelings to glide away into an almost mystical sense of infinity and eternity.

The transformation is however carried not only by the imagery and syntax. The rhyme itself participates in the process. This last stanza stands in distinct contrast to all the previous ones through the assonance of its four last lines. Indeed, these four lines end in sounds distinguishable only by the delicate shading of [çt] vs. [t]. The rhyme words are as follows: *Leid* (whose *d* is pronounced [t]), *steigt* (whose *g* may be pronounced [ç] in harmony with the *ch* of the following rhyme word), *weicht*, and *weit*. The vowel remains the same in all four lines (this alone already sets this stanza apart from the previous ones), and the only slightly varied consonant pattern is thus: [t], [çt], [çt], [t]. A careful analysis thus clearly reveals that the cycle ends with a majestically expanding vision carried organically by the syntax and enhanced by a rhyme structure whose consonant pattern creates a musical confluence of tones, which dissolves all fixed contours. How appropriate, then, that the vowel repeated in these four last lines should be not a vowel at all, but a diphthong—that is, two vowels that are one, or one vowel that is two. The elusive linguistic element of the vowel, itself already more nearly the expression of mood than of contour, appears here in an even *more* evasive form. The ultimate beauty and appropriateness of the diphthong "ei" in this context inheres however in the fact that it is the very embodiment of *motion*. A single vowel such as German *a, e,* or *i* is capable of greatly prolonged, static articulation. Not so the diphthong. If a diphthong is to be articulated at all it must be brought about relatively quickly, the [a] flowing ahead into the [i] to create the dynamic end-product [ai]. Through this happy choice of vowel quality the poet has imbued the expanding vision with an inner life which quite literally overcomes the deadness of earthly gravity and rises dynamically as pure tone.

The cycle, when viewed as a whole, presents a somewhat stereotype story of frustrated desire and suicide, in a rustic setting and drawn directly from the conventions of the "Liederspiel." As such it has a dated charm with a certain popular appeal. Surely it is not this melodramatic aspect which moved a composer of the stature of Schubert to undertake to set the cycle to music. "Die Winterreise," the other Müller cycle which Schubert chose to compose, is lacking in any such simplistic appeal. Clearly there is an aspect in both cycles which lies beneath the surface and which speaks of deeper strata of human experience. It is our contention that a close examination of the more successful poems does indeed yield insights into this underlying meaning, which is at work in the realm of purely lyrical statement behind the often painfully conventional exterior.

In the image of flowing water we have recognized the metaphorical embodiment of a "stream of destiny" which accompanies the boy through life and to which he repeatedly turns for intimations of the meaning and purpose of his wanderings. The dramatic line ascends with the inflation of the boy's hopes and, following the recognition of their illusory nature, begins a descent which is accelerated by outward circumstances (the hunter's entrance) and culminates with the tragic suicide. In the context of this dramatic playlet the hopeless frustrations of life find resolution only in a higher realm beyond death.

The theme of death, when treated not merely as a *topos* but with true organic necessity within a larger context, is of such archetypal relevancy to the human condition that it invariably leads the perceptive reader into the innermost sanctuary of a poet's aesthetic imagination. This is also true in the case of Wilhelm Müller. The moment of death, portrayed in images of quiet majesty and cast in sounds of unusual expressiveness, provides a fitting conclusion to the "Müllerin" cycle and points clearly to the work's underlying poetic content. The problem of death concerned Müller deeply and is treated in a number of the epigrams. We shall look at two of these in order to form a clearer conception of the manner in which the poet approached this central phenomenon. The idea of the individual's destiny, which in the course of the cycle is developed through the symbol of the stream, finds in the moment of death its greatest heightening. The poem "Des

Baches Wiegenlied" portrays death not as the obliteration of consciousness but as a transformation from one state into another. The brook itself remains conscious and ministers to the needs of the sleeper in anticipation of a future awakening ("Bis alles wacht") which is prefigured in the metaphor of the rising moon. From this vantage point Müller's deeper awareness of the theme *Wandern* begins to reveal its significance. Life itself as *Wandern* was for him in the deepest sense a journey into *self-knowledge*. This idea has crystallized into purely conceptual terms in one of the epigrams:

Zwei Reisen

Keine Reis' auf Erden scheint mir so groß und
    schwer zu sein,
Als die Reis' aus uns heraus, als die Reis' in
    uns hinein.[30]

The problem of self-knowledge is here viewed in terms of the theme of wandering. As such it encompasses at the deepest level the mysteries of birth ("in uns hinein") and death ("aus uns heraus"). In the light of this epigram the moment of death is the highest moment of self-knowledge, the goal of the "Wanderschaft" through life, when "... das Meer will trinken die Bächlein aus" ("Des Baches Wiegenlied"). At this moment the spiritual essence of the individual destiny rises as the moon into the cosmic ocean, as a seed of new life.

A clear light is cast upon the mystery by an epigram which was published in the collection "Hundert Sprüche und Sinngedichte" in the year of the poet's own death:

That und Wille

Der Menschenseele gleich in ihres Leibes Hülle,
So wohnt in jeder That des Thäters freier Wille.
Und wann die Todten einst zum neuen Leben gehn,
Wird aus der Thaten Gruft der Wille neu erstehn.[31]

The inner relationship between death and the individuality's freely incurred destiny is here clearly established. The traditional Christian duality of body and soul is employed as a metaphor illustrating Müller's concept of *freedom*. The parallel is meticulously exemplified: just as the *body* is the mortal encasement of the *soul*, so also is human *action* the mortal sheath of the *free will* which in death is liberated from this grave and rises to new life. Despite inner desperation and even the possibility of suicide, death held for Müller a mystery which points to an inner kernel of freedom in the workings of destiny. If we once clearly grasp the scope of Müller's thoughts on death we have found objective verification of what was previously the haunting sensation that there runs underneath the cliché-ridden scenery of this conventional play a current of truly felt concern for the deeper dimensions of life. In the light of the epigrams, the moment of death here portrayed draws back a veil and reveals the secret of our "Wanderschaft," our destiny. The "Reis' aus uns heraus" represented for Müller the greatest enlivening of the process of self-knowledge, in which the free will of man awakens to new life. Müller was concerned with more than harmless clichés when he rounded off his cycle with the line "Und der Himmel da oben, wie ist er so weit!"

It is impossible to say *why* Müller felt moved to work and rework the contents of this conventional "Liederspiel," transforming and enlarging it until it attained its present form. The outer impetus was obviously occasioned by the performance of the earlier traditional version by his circle of friends. The poignancy and depth of the better poems, however, lead us to the conclusion that he was prompted not by the amusing chance concurrence of his name and the miller's role (Müller / Müller), but rather by a dim sensation of the underlying thematics we have examined. The wanderings of the unfortunate miller's boy clearly touched upon a sympathetic fibre in the poet's nature. And the end product had the same effect upon Franz Schubert. Curiously enough, both poet and composer were destined to die while still young men, their wanderings on earth remaining fragmentary. How much, indeed, lies enchanted in the line which every German schoolboy knows by heart:

Das Wandern ist des Müllers Lust!

II

Die Winterreise

A situation outwardly similar to that in "Die schöne Müllerin is presented in "Die Winterreise." The lyrical "I" speaks in the role of a young lover whose rejection by the girl has taken place before the beginning of the cycle. However, the landscape and season reflect an *inner* situation contrasting vividly with the "Müllerin" cycle. The imagery of winter and death which occurred in that cycle only in the poem "Die böse Farbe" forms the context of the entire present work. The poems were largely written and published in the years 1822 and 1823. To these, two more poems were added and the cycle appeared in its final form in volume II of the *Gedichte . . . eines reisenden Waldhornisten*, in 1824.

The Schubert composition, which appeared in 1828, rearranges the order of a number of the songs without seriously affecting the unity of the whole.[1] This points to the basic distinction between this work and the "Müllerin" cycle. Instead of a dramatic curve the "Winterreise" presents a number of basic themes, such as isolation, consuming passion, deception, dream, death-wish. These themes are repeated and varied in the manner of a musical composition of psychological states encompassing the whole scale of emotion from flaming passion to hopelessness. The cycle must thus be viewed with this basic structural principle in mind. The image of the circular motion, which occurs variously in this work, points to the same formal principle. It is therefore quite appropriate to refer to the poems as "Stationen einer Endphase" which are all equally far removed from the "goal," which is of course death and nothingness.[2] The poems of this cycle are closely woven together through images which recur and are transformed. This necessitates an interpretive method which takes nearly all of the poems into consideration, whereas in the case of the other two cycles several largely trite poems may be passed over. A few of the poems in "Die Winterreise" are of particular interest, however, and will be examined closely.

The opening lines of the first poem, "Gute Nacht" (p. 135), are programmatic: "Fremd bin ich eingezogen, / Fremd zieh' ich wieder aus." The image of utter alienation presented here is indeed modern and suggests a reading of the work in "existential" terms.[3] This is certainly true with reference to the central problem of alienation. The situation is however portrayed in terms of a number of very real human emotions, and we therefore find it meaningful to speak also of the *psychological* states involved. We intend the term to be understood not in the sense of the unravelling of motivations in the manner of analytical psychology but in the purely phenomenological sense of observable inner states. This we feel allows for a more exact investigation of the underlying problems than does the mere viewing of the poems as "existential." The two terms will in fact be seen to complement one another.

The poem presents a picture of a man rejected, not only by the girl but by the world. He wanders through darkness and snow accompanied only by his shadow. It is significant that the shadow is cast not by the sun but by the cold light of the moon. The image suggests the tenuousness of the very existence of the lyrical "I" as experienced in these poems. Cast out from human society the wanderer is left without compass-bearings and must find his own way (stanza two), in contrast to the guidance his counterpart received in "Die schöne Müllerin." This engenders in him a temporary feeling of defiance and determination to *choose* his own isolation: "Was soll ich länger weilen, / Bis man mich trieb' hinaus?"

Hence, also, the bitter irony of the line, "Die Liebe liebt das Wandern ... Von Einem zu dem Andern" (stanza three), reminiscent of the irony of "Mein Schatz hat's Grün so gern" ("Die liebe Farbe").

The animal imagery contributes to the mood of grim isolation. The wild animals outside the village might be expected, but even the dogs within the sphere of civilization have become alienated ("irre Hunde"). These dogs, neglected or cast out of human community, represent forcefully the meaningless, lurking danger which may at any moment attack the wanderer.[4]

The act of *writing* the love-message on the gate is an attempt to preserve as outward symbol a proof of an affection which is no longer an unquestioned inner reality. This motif of writing will recur during the cycle and represents a phase in which the question of the bond of love has already become highly problematical.

As the boy begins his journey on foot his eye is caught by a weathervane ("Die Wetterfahne," p. 136). The image is particularly apt, first through the fact that the weathervane is a dead object, and, secondly, in that it is tossed about by an outside force. It is thus immediately seized upon by the boy as a symbol of the state in which he finds himself after the girl has rejected him.

The poem "Gefrorene Thränen" (p. 136) presents the polarity hot/cold which recurs throughout the cycle in the tension between passion and despair. It also portrays the psychological state of insensitivity to one's own emotions: "Und ist's mir denn entgangen, / Daß ich geweinet hab'?" The incorporation of an observation of this psychological complexity into the poem makes amends for the unfortunate image of the rolling ice-tears.[5]

In the more successful poem "Erstarrung" (p. 137) the poet conjures up thoughts of past happiness now withered and gone (Cf. "Trockne Blumen") and is confronted with the icy chill of the present situation. The search for the girl's footprints recalls the writing of the love-message on the gate. It is again the attempt to seize upon an outward *sign* as a token of an experience no longer alive.

The polarity hot/cold presented in the last poem occurs again in a similarly exaggerated form (stanza two). Yet the motif of passion is elaborated in an interesting fashion. The desire to retain a sign or souvenir of the girl's love is justified by the admission that his only tenuous connection with her is maintained through feelings of pain which are transitory: "Wenn meine Schmerzen schweigen, / Wer sagt mir dann von ihr?" The passion of love is now thoroughly infused with the anguish of rejection, and this tortured state of soul drives forth the hot tears.

That the boy feels impelled to preserve a tangible token of his lost joy is in keeping with the psychological-existential crisis of the cycle. Reality has been rent into two extremes and now presents itself to the lyrical "I" only in one of two forms: as the powerful surge of emotion or as the rigidity of death (symbolized by the wintry landscape). As no harmony is forthcoming which might reconcile the opposites, the two sides of the psychological domain must necessarily clash. The outcome of such a conflict within the soul is the loss of any balanced sense of direction. In such a state man is truly "alienated" and can either commit suicide or continue, in blind desperation and out of the stubbornness of his sense of identity, to *wander*. The latter is the path taken in this cycle. Such a treatment of the motif "Wanderschaft" does indeed place these songs in the company of an "existential" outlook well-known in the twentieth century.

In the last stanza we find the motif of the girl's image reflected in the river. This motif, presented in the "Müllerin" cycle in "Thränenregen," appears here in a form appropriate to the new context: "Mein Herz ist wie erfroren, / Kalt starrt ihr Bild darin." In both cases reference is made to "ihr Bild." In "Thränenregen" the image was caught in the water of a flowing brook, and animated reflections merging there united the outer and inner, the dreamlike and "real." In "Erstarrung," however, the poet has through a bold gesture lifted the outer landscape itself, the ice-bound stream, and incorporated it into the wanderer's frozen heart, where it may one day begin to thaw and in its flowing carry away the girl's image: "Schmilzt je das Herz mir wieder, / Fließt auch das Bild dahin." Not only *this* transformation is bold. Whereas the thought of the girl's face mirrored in a flowing stream ("Thränenregen") conforms to all the natural laws of physics and optics, the notion of such an image becoming in a sense permanently "fixed" (I borrow the term from the photographer's darkroom) in the ice, though psychologically and metaphorically sound, clearly *violates* these laws, and can justifiably be called daring.

In the present passage the boy's inner life, the heart itself, has frozen solid in harmony with outer nature, and erected an invisible barrier which precludes the possibility of any poetic union with the girl's image. The memory picture held within this frozen heart is again a dead "sign" entirely analogous to that written on the gate, that left in the form of footprints, or that which we shall soon see the wanderer inscribe into the ice.

"Der Lindenbaum" (p. 137) is one of the most beloved "folksongs" in the German-speaking world and has so established itself in the consciousness of the populace that the author's identity is often forgotten. It is the most important poem in "Die Winterreise" and will therefore be discussed in detail.

The linden tree, a popular species in German folk poetry,[6] calls forth past memories in the poet: "Ich träumt' in seinem Schatten / So manchen süßen Traum." The isolation of winter wandering is here broken through by a "sweet dream." The sphere of the tree will recur in "Rückblick" and "Frühlingstraum" and represents a familiar, homelike spot at which the wanderer may recuperate from the turbulent experiences of the outer world. In the shade of the tree the young man feels protected, and it is thus not surprising that he also feels *drawn* to the tree, wherever he may be. Near it he finds the peace of mind which allows hidden wishes and dreams to well up within his soul. It is no accident that Müller has chosen the "Brunnenlinde," characteristic of so many German villages, as the special focal point of the wanderer's longings. We recognize in the fountain an image reminiscent of the poetic world of the "Müllerin" cycle. It is a source of water flowing forth out of the dark earth, as in "Wohin?" ("Wohl aus dem Felsenquell"). In the language of metaphor it is once again the wellspring of the imaginative, inner world as we have discussed it in the last chapter. At this spot in the soul-landscape of the "Winterreise" the linden tree grows. It is thus in an even deeper sense understandable that a dream-like atmosphere emanates from this place. Tree and fountain are significantly located "vor dem Thore"—i.e., outside of the confines of the town. The spatial arrangement of the scenery is thus an exact correlative for the relationship between two states of consciousness—the everyday world of waking life and the world of dreams which is approached upon falling asleep, as through a gate.

In the shadow of the tree the wanderer feels enveloped by a protective, dreamlike veil and begins to perceive a magical language which surrounds him. It is a gentle whispering out of which there soon speaks a message of sweet temptation, promising *rest* ("Ruh'," stanza four). The wanderer is in danger of being drawn back into blissful memories, dreams of past happiness. But the word "Ruh'" has a ring so deep and mysterious that it at the same time promises an ultimate rest, in death. Now we understand this poem's perennial appeal, for it speaks not only of everyday occurrences but simultaneously of the age-old questions of life and death. The sphere of the homey and familiar village linden tree is thus expanded into a new dimension. On this second level the locale represents pictorially a dividing-line in the soul-landscape. It is a spot within consciousness at which the lyrical "I" is exposed to the mysterious and dangerous whisperings of a dream world which would entice it into giving up the struggle for life. The power of this temptation is rendered doubly intense through the personal identification with the tree established by the "liebe Worte" carved into its bark by the wanderer. His deepest feelings have hereby been physically inscribed in the tree and henceforth will exert a powerful magnetic force upon his soul: "Es zog in Freud' und Leide / Zu ihm mich immer fort." The totality of the boy's psychological commitment to this place comes to expression in the characteristically polar formula "Freud' und Leid," which we have discussed in the previous chapter ("Des Baches Wiegenlied"). In the face of such a powerful temptation within the soul, the wanderer must seek to maintain his wakefulness and thereby also his identity. This is the struggle portrayed in the further course of the poem.

We shall now proceed to trace the oscillation between temptation and self-assertion in the poem as a whole. The first two stanzas present the sphere of the tree, as discussed above. This is followed in stanza three by the wanderer's description of his most recent encounter with the tree: "Ich mußt' auch heute wandern / Vorbei in tiefer Nacht." The awareness of danger comes to expression not only through the word "mußt'" and the nocturnal atmosphere but is also suggested through the closing of the eyes. There is clearly no objective reason for our wanderer to close his eyes when the darkness of night surrounds him anyway. He seeks to remain unaffected by the mysterious force of the tree by blocking it out of his field of vision entirely. The ear is not as easily closed as is the eye however, and an acoustical impression causes the pendulum to swing back to the realm of temptation, in stanza four: "Und seine Zweige rauschten, / Als riefen sie mir zu." We are again back in the force-field of the tree which proceeds to whisper "Komm her zu mir, Geselle, / Hier findst du deine Ruh'!" The word "Geselle" appears in a similar connection in "Rückblick" (stanza four) and points to the idyllic, homelike sphere of the tree. This pleasant mood is however simultaneously shot through with the magical enticement of the rustling branches.

The familiar elements of the other cycle now appear once more. The key word is "rauschten," which in German is applicable both to the rustling of leaves and the rushing of water. Through this word, the associations of a "watery" (i.e., dreamlike) nature saturate the entire atmosphere surrounding the tree. They contrast vigorously with the feeling of hard, unmoving ice which during the entire cycle symbolizes the isolation of the wanderer's soul. The similarity of the present stanza with stanza five of "Wohin?" is striking:

> Was sag' ich denn vom Rauschen?
> Das kann kein Rauschen sein:
> Es singen wohl die Nixen
> Dort unten ihren Reihn.   ("Wohin?")
>
> Und seine Zweige rauschten,
> Als riefen sie mir zu:
> Komm her zu mir, Geselle,
> Hier findst du deine Ruh'!   ("Lindenbaum")

The word "Geselle" in turn recalls a similar line in "Thränenregen": "Geselle, Geselle, mir nach!" The last line of the above stanza could just as well have been spoken by the stream in the other cycle:

> "Des Baches Wiegenlied": Gute Ruh', gute Ruh'!
> Thu' die Augen zu!
>
> "Der Lindenbaum":   Hier findst du deine Ruh'!

These parallels are not accidental. This is the one spot in the "Winterreise" at which the lyrical "I" is directly exposed to the enticing world of enchantment and dream, symbolized by the verb "rauschen."

In stanza five the pendulum swings back again to the isolated "I," which defies the danger and seeks to maintain itself against wind and cold: "Der Hut flog mir vom Kopfe, / Ich wendete mich nicht."

In the last stanza the temporal progression, having moved first through a distant, then a near past, finally reaches the present. The spatial designation has similarly developed from an imaginative proximity to the tree to an actual physical separation which is of course implied during the entire poem. Nevertheless, this separation has no real meaning, for the "Rauschen" has meanwhile slipped into the wanderer's soul, where it continues to sound: "Und immer hör' ich's rauschen:

/ Du fändest Ruhe dort!" The outer tree serves to occasion a deeper *inner* experience which lives on within the soul. The scope of this experience comes to expression in the choice of words. The pronoun "Du" is of course directed by the animated "Rauschen" to the poet-wanderer, through the latter's inner ear. Through the operation of the "lyrical I," however, the reader feels it to be directed to himself as well. The word "dort" is even more mysterious. If it is simply an unspecified rustling voice which calls to mind the tree, then the word "dort" merely signifies this tree. But it can just as well be the remembered "voice" of the tree itself, rustling within the wanderer's soul. If this is the case and the voice is directed by the tree toward the wanderer's consciousness, then it can no longer point to the *tree* as the place of eternal rest, for in order to do so it would have to say not "dort" but "hier," as indeed it does in stanza four. The word is, happily, very unspecific in its reference. As the final word in the poem it leaves open an infinity of possible associations, such as "fountain," "rushing water," "rustling leaves," and "death." This is of course entirely appropriate to the whole conception of the poem and of both song-cycles, for the ultimate rest ("Ruhe") of which the rustling tree whispers is to be found only in the realm of eternity.

The phenomenon of release, of dissolving into eternity as expressed in the last stanza of "Des Baches Wiegenlied" through the image of the moonrise and the musicality of the language, is presented here as a temptation which approaches the wanderer through a metamorphosis of the spatial-temporal into an *inner* world of the soul. (The details of this metamorphosis we shall trace shortly.) The wanderer is then confronted with the choice of struggling on in the meaningless isolation in which he finds himself (metaphorically: ice) or of succumbing to the temptation to give up the urge to maintain his individual identity and simply to slip away into the peace of the beyond ("dort," metaphorically: water). It is a choice between two extremes, neither of which is ultimately favorable to life. The greatness of this little poem lies just in the *tension* so keenly felt by a man who is unable to harmonize these two extremes within his soul.

The alternation of moods in the song may be represented schematically as follows:

        stanza 1:   tree - temptation
        stanza 2:   tree - temptation
        stanza 3:   "I" - self-assertion
        stanza 4:   tree - temptation
        stanza 5:   "I" - self-assertion
        stanza 6:   tree - temptation

Schubert composes stanzas 1, 2, 4, and 6 in a major key and stanzas 3 and 5 in a minor key, whereby the music corresponds precisely to the changes in content. The unresolved psychological tension rendered visually tangible through the metaphors of the "watery" vs. the "icy" realms impinging upon consciousness thus finds further embodiment in the poem's formal structure. This occurs first in the above-mentioned alternation of mood between major and minor keys and secondly in the more finite detail of the rhythmical juxtaposition of feminine and masculine rhymes. A shimmering oscillation underlies the entire poetic statement.

The tension in question is heightened by the progressive transformation of time and space into the interior world of the wanderer's soul. We have alluded to this transformation above and are now in a position to describe it fully.

The use of *time* within the poem is introduced in the first two lines with the present tense reference to the tree. The narrative then shifts into the past tense as the speaker recounts his various experiences in the vicinity of the tree. Therefore it is clear that while the two introductory lines are given in the present tense, the wanderer's relationship to the tree is no longer a present one. The adverb "da" ("Da steht ein Lindenbaum") suggests that the thought of the tree is drawn from out of the memory. In stanzas three, four, and five the past has drawn closer ("Ich mußt' auch heute wandern"), and the last stanza is cast in the present tense. Although lines one and two of the first stanza stand *grammatically* in the present, they are from the standpoint of *content* clearly rooted in the past. The only lines in the poem which are not drawn from memory are those of the final stanza. It is now important to note that it is actually only the first two lines ("Nun bin ich manche Stunde / Entfernt von jenem Ort") which are in the strict sense conceived in the present. The following two ("Und immer hör' ich's rauschen: / Du fändest Ruhe dort") report an acoustical perception which is, to be sure, presently heard, but which at the same time is so internalized that it melts together and unites with the memories of the past. As we have seen, it is a rustling voice which speaks *now* about a specific tree as a locus of peace ("dort"), but it is *simultaneously*—and hereby the experience is vastly deepened—the voice of the rustling tree itself, which now is remembered ("erinnert") and reëchoes from out of the past within the wanderer's soul. The experiences of the past now well up in recollection and are therefore active in the present, but in a completely internalized form.

The use of *space* rests upon the same principle. In the first stanza the tree seems to be only a short distance from the speaker ("Da steht ein Lindenbaum"), and, indeed, our sense of its presence is entirely justified; for only in the last stanza do we realize that it is very far away. The memory-picture presented in the opening stanza conveys the distinct impression of nearness to the speaker. In the last stanza the distance is indicated by more than the vague "da": "Nun bin ich manche Stunde / Entfernt von jenem Ort." Once we have arrived at the end of the poem and look back from this vantage point we realize that the entire poem is conceived in the present moment and right "here," at a great distance from the tree. This realization can only be had now, at the *end* of the poem. Despite the grammatical present of the introductory lines the experienced content moves in a recollected progression from the past and the distant to the temporally and spatially present. By the end of the poem, both principles (time and space) have transmuted themselves into the inner life of the speaker. The phenomenon is wondrous enough when one considers that in lyric poetry of this sort the outward landscape is *already* a soul-landscape spread out around the lyrical "I."

Here we see certain elements of this soul-landscape metamorphose themselves and find their way right into the living kernel of this "I" itself. The "then" and "there" of experiences stored up in this soul-landscape as *memory* have hereby become "now" and "here" in the psychological-existential struggles presently taking place in the innermost sanctuary of the "I." This soul now experiences inwardly not only the frozen image of the past in a "frozen heart" ("Erstarrung") but also the internalized world of the rustling tree. If it seemed surprising to us to encounter the incorporation of the icy river into the very heart of the speaker himself ("Erstarrung," stanza five), we have here simply the complementary incorporation of the tree and all that is associated with it *into* the heart and soul of the speaker. And the spatial concept ends oddly enough with the paradoxical word "dort," so that the internalization of space even contains its potentially unlimited psychological expansion as a temptation.

No harmonizing synthesis between "I" and world is presented in the poem. The opposite spheres of the isolated self vs. the hostile world, of the necessity to maintain identity and the danger of being tempted to give up, remain unreconciled. The wanderer's soul gathers up experiences and feelings from out of his memory and in so doing allows them to come to life in the innermost sanctuary of his heart. By finding their way into the creative center of the "I" the existential problems grow greatly in intensity and immediacy—to the distress of the wanderer and to the obvious benefit of the poem as an aesthetic statement.

The true nature of the two threats which confront the wanderer now becomes evident. Either force, if allowed to overpower the soul, will lead to death. It is eminently characteristic that Müller's tendency to view the world in terms of polarities should come to expression in his view of the question of the spiritual death of his wanderer. Death approaches him on the one side as radical psychological isolation (Cf. "Der greise Kopf," "Die Krähe") and on the other hand lurks behind the temptation to flee into a formless "dort," the eternal rest of which the stream in "Des Baches

Wiegenlied" has sung: "Gute Ruh', gute Ruh'! / Thu' die Augen zu!" These two threats to man's existence are woven into each of the cycles as metaphors through the element in nature which in each case predominates: in the "Müllerin" as water and in the "Winterreise" as ice. It is the same *element*, which appears in two different *states*—in the first cycle formless, in the second radically frozen in form.

Since in the remainder of the cycle the wanderer continues to give himself over to the sphere of icy loneliness and despair, it is possible to view "Der Lindenbaum" as the actual "heart" of the work. In this poem the problem of human existence is examined in terms of the polarity of ultimate dangers to the soul in a manner which is unique within the cycle. Schubert has enlivened and clarified this polarity, as noted above, in the encompassing *musical* equivalent of contrasting major and minor keys. This musical handling recurs in the composition of the song "Frühlingstraum," which appears as a gentle echo of "Der Lindenbaum." In "Frühlingstraum," however, the depth of the problem of death is no longer touched upon. The minor key is predominant in the cycle, both before and after "Der Lindenbaum." As the actual "heart" of the cycle, "Der Lindenbaum" points to a deep riddle of existence. The peculiar fascination of this poem derives from the tension with which the wanderer must struggle and the embodiment of this tension thematically, metaphorically, formally, and (with the help of Schubert) even musically. As long as such a polarity of inner experience can still be held more or less in balance, the human being can continue to breathe and to live. It is therefore not inappropriate that the poem's title and central motif is an image of pure vegetative life: "Der Lindenbaum."

The wanderer's hopeful gaze sweeps for a moment back to the world of human community in the poem "Die Post" (p. 138). The rhythm of the postman's galloping horse, imitated through the four-beat iambic couplets, imparts a sense of excitement to the poem. Against the background of this galloping rhythm the refrain "Mein Herz?" sounds forth rather as the blast of the postal horn itself. The messenger from town awakens in the wanderer both memories and hopes centering around the girl. But although the winter is here not even mentioned, the sense of separation is retained by a subtle detail: the only possible contact with the girl is suggested through the intermediary of the horn, which is itself a dead object. And the suggestion of such a contact is not even taken seriously by the boy himself: "Die Post bringt keinen Brief für dich." The impossibility of the situation is heightened by the refrain "Mein Herz?" which is a question directed by the questioner to himself. Only in stanza three is the question mark replaced by an exclamation point. This momentary sense of certainty immediately snaps back into the picture of the ego posing hopeless questions to itself. Since all hopes are in vain the effect of the rising emotions is hollow, and in the following poem the melancholia again pours into the disillusioned soul.

The relationship between heart and ice, established in stanza five of "Erstarrung," appears transformed in "Auf dem Flusse" (p. 139). Whereas in the former poem the ice which held the girl's image was incorporated into the *inward* realm of the heart, the present poem presents the opposite situation: the wanderer engraves a memento of the girl into the ice of the river *outside* and then sees in it an image of his heart: "Mein Herz, in diesem Bache, / Erkennst du nun dein Bild?"

The first stanza appears as a variation of the situation in "Wohin?" The rushing water has been silenced by the cold. The stream which is felt as a guiding force has fallen completely dumb and lies stretched out motionless in the sand.

The themes from earlier poems are now recurring almost in the manner of transformed leitmotifs. In this sense the act of *writing* introduced in "Der Lindenbaum" reappears in "Auf dem Flusse" in variation. The boy now writes not in the bark of the tree but into the icy surface of the river. Appropriately enough, the *content* of the written message appears in the present less dreamy poem in a much more sharply contoured form. Instead of the vague "So manches liebe Wort" the wanderer now writes a singularly precise bit of information: "Den Namen meiner Liebsten / Und Stund'

und Tag..." It is here no longer love in general, but very *specific moments* which he seeks to preserve in this artificial manner. In this sense this painfully time-conscious message is of course the exact *opposite* of the timeless love it seeks to symbolize. The entire love experience has here contracted into a few words. These little "signs" are a pathetic remnant of past happiness and will disappear with the thawing of the dead ice into which they have been scratched. This employment of "signs" and "letters" contrasts strikingly to their use in the cycle "Frühlingskranz," in which they are very much alive, as we shall see.

A ring reminiscent of Eichendorff's "zerbrochenes Ringlein" is now drawn around these signs in the attempt to hold together the passing experience of love with the archetypal symbol of timelessness. The moment represented by the date was to be eternalized through this procedure, but the impossibility of the attempt, which has itself fallen victim to the time-bound activity of writing, finds its necessary symbolic expression: the ring is broken. In the face of this hopeless situation the poet turns in the final stanza to a contemplation of the tearing pain of emotion within his heart. This is presented through the comparison with the waters under the icy cover of the river, and the attentive reader may have noticed that the cutting sensation of pain is driven home through a most extraordinarily subtle device. It is the introduction of the phrase "Mein Herz...?" which hearkens back to the poem "Die Post," in which, in its function as tortured refrain, it sounded forth with all the piercing force of the posthorn itself, penetrating the cold night air.

The poems "Rückblick" (p. 139) and "Der greise Kopf" (p. 140) complement one another in that the first focuses attention on the past and the second on the future. Through the fond memories of past happiness which arise within the wanderer's recollection, the motifs of "Der Lindenbaum" are touched upon in "Rückblick." The odd use of bird imagery is striking in the poem. The notion of crows throwing hail at the fleeing boy from every house has been explained by one critic as "ein halluzinatorisches Bild."[7] This "explanation" is nevertheless not an interpretation and simply dismisses the image without contributing to its clarification. A key to its meaning is provided in another of Müller's poems, "Heimkehr" (Hatfield, p. 140). In this poem the birds are employed as symbols of the poet's thoughts and feelings which flutter about and finally come to rest on the girl's house. This is clearly the sense in which the image of the crows is employed in "Rückblick." The wanderer feels himself to be driven out of town and mocked by a series of beings which actually give pictorial expression to his own inner state.

It should now no longer surprise us to find that even such a motif as the birds is experienced as a polarity. With the reawakening of fond memories (stanza three) there appear the lark and nightingale. They are no more "hallucinatory" than the crows but are in a real sense their opposite, for they belong in the soul-landscape of spring as this arises in memory.

The remembered world of spring is the world of the "Müllerin" cycle, with its bubbling brook instead of ice and snow. The epithet "glühend" applied to the girl's eyes has appeared twice already in the "Winterreise" to characterize tears.[8] In contrast to the cold, it consistently denotes burning emotion.

With the appearance of the sweet memories there is aroused in the wanderer's soul the old temptation to retreat into the past—this time, however, in a much less radical form than in "Der Lindenbaum": "Kömmt mir der Tag in die Gedanken, / Möcht' ich noch einmal rückwärts sehn." It is here merely the retrospective contemplation of a past happy day. There is no intimation of eternal rest.

In "Der greise Kopf" (p. 140) the gaze is directed towards the future, and the longing for death increases in intensity. The disillusionment with life is denoted by the boy's strange brooding on the frost which has settled on his head and which gives the appearance of the advanced age which he would welcome were it only forthcoming. The wish to sink back into the past ("Der Lindenbaum," "Rückblick") is here complemented by a desire to rush *forward* into death. The effect produced by the thought of a young man who dwells on such ideas is grim indeed. Schubert's treatment of the poem underscores this most forcefully. In the line "Wie weit noch bis zur Bahre!" he uses an atonal device which seems to anticipate some twentieth-century modes of composition. Transplanted into his world of otherwise very harmonious tones it has the ring of a tortured cry.[9]

The next two poems center on the mood of hopelessness which erodes the wanderer's entire being. One of the crows from "Rückblick" appears in "Die Krähe" (p. 140) as the personification of the thoughts of meaninglessness and of death. The crow describes eerie circles in the air, and the rotating motion so beautifully captured by Schubert is suggested in the repetition "für und für." In stanza two the thought of death is further developed in a way entirely in keeping with the psychological realities of this cycle. The wanderer here contemplates death by focusing his attention on its *physical* aspect alone. The image of death here contracts into the picture of a corpse: "Meinst wohl bald als Beute hier / Meinen Leib zu fassen?"

The last stanza gives a bitterly ironic twist to the theme of "Wanderschaft," which in the romantic sense implies a longing which draws one into far distant domains, ultimately into a spiritual "beyond." In this poem the "beyond" is actually a nothingness, a *néant*. This is a theme reminiscent of an "existential" view developed in the twentieth century. In keeping with this transformation of the theme of wandering the other central theme of fidelity finds its correspondingly warped form in the identification of the crow with what ought to have been the fidelity of a loved one. In this sense it is quite correct to speak of the crows as "pervertierte ... Sinnfiguren der Treue."[10]

In "Letzte Hoffnung" (p. 141) the monotony suggested in the last poem by the circling of the crow is expressed by the repetition of the same rhyme-word in the first and third lines of each stanza. The wanderer's flagging hope is attached to the metaphor of the last leaf which still clings to the twig, tossed about by the wind as was the weathervane in "Die Wetterfahne."

The poem's placement within the cycle's structure is of

interest. It is the twelfth of twenty-four poems and does indeed represent a turning point. It serves as a last, trembling link to the experiences of the past, and is thus beautifully reflected in the metaphor of the last leaf. In "Frühlingstraum" this past is touched upon once again, but in a transformed dream state. The only concrete reference to the past (such as in "Die Post" or the reminiscences in a waking state in "Rückblick") which will occur in the remainder of the cycle is the allusion to the girl's eyes in "Die Nebensonnen," and this allusion is itself merely a well-concealed *topos*.

Just as the first half of the cycle ended with two poems centering on the mood of hopelessness, the second half now opens with two poems embodying a mood of turbulence and haste.

In characteristic fashion, Müller again employs a contrast of opposite states of mind in order to emphasize the one with which he is presently concerned. In "Im Dorfe" (p. 141) the theme of dream, already handled in "Der Lindenbaum," serves as a foil whereby to accentuate the vividly awake state of isolation in which the wanderer finds himself. Other men may sleep, passing through the world of dreams (polarity: "Thun sich im Guten und Argen erlaben"), while he is forced to remain awake. The world of dreams, into which the denizens of the village plunge in sleep, is here once again associated with the watery element through the choice of verb: "Und morgen früh ist Alles zerflossen."

With the reintroduction of the image of dogs, already presented in "Gute Nacht," another secret of the composition of the cycle is revealed. As the thirteenth of twenty-four poems, "Im Dorfe" represents the introductory poem of the second half of the cycle, whereas "Gute Nacht" introduces the first half. It is thus interesting that the dogs are reintroduced in just this poem, in the manner of an octave. The difference in their expressive function, however, points to the heightening in the emotional scale which we are observing between the two pairs of poems separated by the turning point in the center of the cycle (hopelessness in "Die Krähe" and "Letzte Hoffnung," as compared with feverish haste in "Im Dorfe" and the following poem, "Der stürmische Morgen"). In "Gute Nacht" the dogs are described as "irre Hunde" whereas in "Im Dorfe" we hear of "wache Hunde." The heightening is obvious—the dogs have become more active and purposeful and seem to drive the wanderer out of town. The dogs will reappear as a "second octave" in a particularly disturbing image in the last poem of the cycle.

The formal structure of "Im Dorfe" again reveals Müller's aesthetic sensitivity in the contrasting length of the two stanzas. The second stanza must be only half the length of the first, for it represents a shift from a relatively passive, descriptive stance (stanza one: third person) to an active conversation with the dogs (stanza two: second person). The tragic isolation felt within the soul here increases in intensity as the wanderer rushes out of town, and this condensation of anxiety finds formal expression in the compressed length of the second stanza. The thematics of this stanza underscore the conscious desire *not* to rest. The wanderer's isolation increases with the rejection of all contact with his fellow men ("Was will ich unter den Schläfern säumen?") as he thrusts ahead in blind resignation toward the grave. In this consciously willed, frozen alienation of the individual self we can begin to see the problem of death in this cycle take on a form which might be likened to an absolute zero-point of isolation.

The burning anguish of "Rückblick" ("Es brennt mir unter beiden Sohlen") appears intensified in "Der stürmische Morgen" (p. 142) in the powerful imagery of the stormy sky. At this point the first true color to be introduced in the cycle makes its appearance. It is the most vivid color in the spectrum, red, which here strikes into the heart of the cycle in the flash of lightning. The wintry sky is personified and the clouds described as its shredded garment. We shall observe this tendency of Müller's to personify natural phenomena as it is employed in quite a different manner in the cycle "Frühlingskranz."

The use of the stormy sky as a reflection of a state of soul is clarified through a comparison with the last stanza of "Auf dem Flusse":

> Mein Herz, in diesem Bache
> Erkennst du nun dein Bild?
> Ob's unter seiner Rinde
> Wohl auch so reißend schwillt?
> ("Auf dem Flusse")

> Mein Herz sieht an dem Himmel
> Gemalt sein eignes Bild -
> Es ist nichts als der Winter,
> Der Winter kalt und wild!
> ("Der stürmische Morgen")

The turmoil of anguish dimly sensed as present underneath the solid ice-covering of the river is here clearly seen in greatly expanded dimensions as a violent meteorological upheaval spread out upon the heavens themselves. The refrain "Mein Herz," which pulsates through "Die Post," is once again reintroduced as the opening words of the last stanza of another poem, and links the above two stanzas formally as well as thematically. This is another example of the delicate reawakening of themes and motifs in the course of the cycle which gives the entire work its peculiarly musical quality. The fact that the imagery associated with the words has transformed itself from one poem to another points to the vitality of the cycle's content—a vitality rendered all the more vibrant through the contrasting devices consciously introduced by the author to suggest monotony (weathervane, circling crows, repetition of words, etc.).

The three following poems pick up the central theme of "Wanderschaft," interweaving it with those of deception and death. The introduction in "Täuschung" (p. 142) of the will-o'-the-wisp is particularly striking. The attentive reader may sense the delicate thread connecting this poem to the foregoing one through the use of the phenomenon of light. We mean here not light as backdrop or general illumination of the scene, but light as an active detail inserted into the scene against a larger backdrop. The will-o'-the-wisp, dancing and darting about ahead of the wanderer, appears here as a pale after-image of the flash of lightning breaking forth from the unruly cloudscape of "Der stürmische Morgen." At the same time the dancing light anticipates the poem "Irrlicht," which occurs later in the cycle and with which the will-o'-the-wisp is identified through the theme of deception. Through these inner links in imagery and theme the poem is thus woven into the larger fabric of the cycle. The theme of enticement (*Lockung*), so often associated with the element of water, appears here attached to the will-o'-the-wisp. The mutually shared quality in both cases is that of *formlessness*. The nixie-like temptations of the light ("Ich folg' ihm gern, und seh's ihm an, / Daß es verlockt den Wandersmann") recall to mind the enticements of the water-spirits in the "Müllerin" cycle. They are able to becloud the wanderer's consciousness through their flitting, darting motion which is not unlike the jumping and tumbling of the water of the brook. There is one crucial difference, however—the distinction between auditory and visual perception. In the present poem there is no mention of spirit voices. The wanderer is attracted and led astray purely by the flickering of the light. The difference points to a very deep distinction between the two situations. The nixie voices in the water, in such a poem as "Thränenregen" ("Geselle, Geselle, mir nach!") or in the watery *Rauschen* of the leaves of the "Lindenbaum," seem to tone forth from out of mysterious, unseen depths. Carried on the waves of sound, they find easy access through the ear of man and echo within the hidden recesses of the soul. Not so the temptations of the will-o'-the-wisp. The impression here is entirely visual and as such much more manageable. It cannot gain access to the wanderer's soul with such insidious penetration as could the auditory impressions. (We recall the fact that in "Der Lindenbaum" the wanderer is able to block out visual impressions by shutting his eyes as he passes the tree, whereas its rustling continues to slip into his soul.) The result of this difference is that while he is enticed to follow the dancing of the light, the wanderer maintains a great deal more distance from the phenomenon than was possible in the case of the auditory attacks. Thus he is able to be tempted by the dancing of the little light and at the same time, quite literally, *"see* it for what it is," a "bunte List": "Ach, wer wie ich so elend ist, / Giebt gern sich hin der bunten List." This in turn enables him to maintain his identity, for he realizes that this spirit-temptation can for him only represent illusion (*Täuschung*). The conclusion is then drawn: "Nur Täuschung ist für mich Gewinn!" The statement represents a disillusioned soul's conscious embracing of illusion and as such has the ring of sophistry about it. Disenchantment with his state drives him to follow the lead of the flitting light, even though the fact that he clearly knows that the spirit's enticements are illusory robs them of their occult force. The psychological state here described is complex indeed and underscores through its quality of intellectual detachment the sense of the isolation of soul which is of course accompanied by one-sided wakefulness rather than dreamlike trance.

The mood of isolation is further intensified in "Der Wegweiser" (p. 142) through the lonely mountain landscape, while the theme of wandering is clearly placed against the background of inner compulsion: "Eine Straße muß ich gehen, / Die noch Keiner ging zurück." The poem turns on the employment of the images of roadsign and road which are linked metaphorically with the theme of death. The quality of sincerity which pervades the poem is enriched by the agonizing self-questioning of the first two stanzas. Unable to explain his actions, the wanderer asks himself *why* he must avoid more travelled roads and why he should feel driven along into isolation, not having committed any misdeeds. This agonizing introspection contrasts rather sharply with the boy's self-questioning in the "Müllerin" cycle. There the process involved a listener—the brook, as a guiding force directly sensed. In the present poem, however, he is thrown back upon himself with his hopeless questions and is thereby driven all the more forcefully into isolation, despair, and death.

In "Das Wirthshaus" (p. 143) the theme of wandering is further heightened through a protracted metaphorical association with that of death. The central themes are complemented by several motifs already familiar to us from earlier poems so that the total effect is one of musicality.

The word "Weg," picked up from the previous poem, occurs in line two as the subject of a sentence whose direct object is the wanderer himself: "Auf einen Todtenacker / Hat mich mein Weg gebracht." Used in this manner the "path" is experienced as an active agent which leads man to his ultimate goal. An inkling of the notion of a hidden guiding force in life, reminiscent of the brook in the "Müllerin," is touched on by this conception.

The funeral wreaths (stanza two) combine two metaphors with which we are familiar. The first is the broken ring of "Auf dem Flusse" which appears now closed as a symbol of eternity in death. The second is the color green whose deep metaphorical association with death was developed in "Die liebe Farbe" ("Die schöne Müllerin"). This color and the red of "Der stürmische Morgen" are the only colors which light up against the otherwise entirely gray and white background of this cycle. The green will appear once more in "Frühlingstraum" in association with dreams of new life—once again the polar opposite meaning.

The inn, a favorite romantic locale, is employed in this poem in ironic transformation as the place whose rooms (graves) offer the tired wanderer ultimate rest.

The use of the grammatical person in this poem is interesting. The third person (stanza one, lines one and two), which describes the poet's having been led to the cemetery, is succeeded by two lines of reaction in the first person. These lines express acceptance of the situation. The following three stanzas all employ the second person, as the poet addresses first the wreaths, then the cemetery ("inn") itself, and finally the walking-stick. The third person of the poem's beginning yields to a tone which through the wanderer's questions becomes increasingly intimate until in the last stanza he is rejected and the second person address is directed to his closest friend in distress, the faithful walking-stick. The old theme of "Wandern-Müssen," coupled here with the ironic variation on the theme of fidelity (Cf. "Die Krähe"), casts the boy back into the world. That he should now address the walking-stick as "mein treuer Wanderstab" is particularly poignant in that the only "friend" with whom he can converse is a piece of dead wood.

The motif of the will-o'-the-wisp ("Täuschung") is reintroduced in "Das Irrlicht" (p. 143), in which the mood of resignation in the face of illusion has been intensified to one of utter apathy. The entire gamut of human experience (polarity again: "Unsre Freuden, unsre Wehen") appears now as ultimately meaningless. It is thus out of a deep artistic necessity that the poet chooses the imagery of the third stanza—the dry bed of the mountain stream. The whole living being of the mountain brook, with all its associations as presented in "Die schöne Müllerin," has "died" and left behind it only a "corpse." The last two lines of "Das Irrlicht" contain in jewel-like distillation pictures of death which are drawn from the core of the imaginative world of each cycle. The first of these two, "Jeder Strom wird's Meer gewinnen" recalls vividly to mind the death-metaphor in the last song of the "Müllerin," "Das Baches Wiegenlied": "Bis das Meer will trinken die Bächlein aus." The second of the two lines, "Jedes Leiden auch ein Grab," presents a picture of death no longer viewed in terms of transcendent expansion but rather of physical collapse, centered at a definite point in space, the grave (the image introduced in "Das Wirthshaus"). The contrast in the experience of the confrontation with death as portrayed in the two cycles is aptly symbolized in the images of *ocean* and *grave*.

The mood of apathy in "Das Irrlicht," if allowed to establish itself firmly in the soul, quickly leads to a laming of the whole being. In "Rast" (p. 144) this paralysis descends upon our wanderer: "Nun merk' ich erst, wie müd' ich bin, / Da ich zur Ruh' mich lege." Feelings of this sort have made themselves known earlier, as in "Das Wirthshaus": "Bin matt zum Niedersinken / Und tödtlich schwer verletzt." The wanderer is increasingly consumed by them. Indeed, the word "consumed" points to a metaphor of unusual profundity which is introduced in this poem. The wanderer finds lodging and a fitful rest in the little house of a charcoal-burner. Stanza three describes the pause:

> In eines Köhlers engem Haus
> Hab' Obdach ich gefunden;
> Doch meine Glieder ruhn nicht aus:
> So brennen ihre Wunden.

The wanderer here describes quite vividly the burning of his wounds, which precludes the chance for any true rest. The searing ache of a wounded heart (stanza four) which has driven the wanderer across the miles has by now worked its way down into the physical organism itself. The body craves rest but is pushed on beyond its power of endurance by a soul not at peace. The result is that even the physical body is consumed by the process ("So brennen ihre Wunden"). The ultimate outcome of this process is the longed-for death. But the charcoal-burner is himself a man who by profession watches over just such a burning process, whereby living matter is transformed through slow combustion into black, dead material. Whether he knew it consciously or not (and it is possible that he did) Müller has here touched upon a metaphor of uncanny appropriateness to the theme of the poem.

The choice of the title "Rast" points to the fact that the longed-for "Ruhe" is still unattainable and that this rest can therefore only be momentary. In direct allusion to the imagery of "Der stürmische Morgen" the heart is described as filled with emotion which will drive the boy onward: "Auch du, mein Herz, im Kampf und Sturm / So wild und so verwegen."

The theme of illusion, attached already to the image of light in the form of the will-o'-the-wisps, now invades the very archetypal source of light itself—the sun ("Die Nebensonnen," p. 144). The preoccupation with meaninglessness and death leads ultimately to the point at which even the highest life-giving entity appears in a distorted form. It is thus entirely appropriate that this poem's form should break with the "Volksliedstrophe" as did also that of "Täuschung."

Both of these poems, which in a central way treat of the theme of illusion, are cast in a single ten-line, four-beat iambic stanza. The rhyme is handled in couplets, rather than in the more freely flowing patterns *a b a b* or *a b c b* which characterize most of the poems in the cycle. The rhyme is also masculine throughout. The result is that these two poems are embodied in a form whose static, heavy quality most fittingly complements the brooding preoccupation with illusion which they describe.

The childlike rejection of the vision of the mock suns ("Ach, *meine* Sonnen seid ihr nicht!") hearkens back directly to the poem "Des Müllers Blumen," in which a corresponding positive reaction to the flowers which resemble the girl's eyes is expressed: "Drum sind es meine Blumen." The similarity of these two reactions is grounded in a common metaphor, for in the two mock suns we have a *topos* for the girl's eyes, as is evident from the boy's lamentation over the loss of two of "his" suns: "Ja, neulich hatt' ich auch wohl drei: Nun sind hinab die besten zwei." The final two lines express the wish that the "third" (i.e., the real) sun might also disappear, for, in the absence of the other two, the world about were better dark. Forgetting, darkness and death are all that seems meaningful now.

In "Frühlingstraum" (p. 144) a dream of spring represents one last moment of inner warmth before the end of the cycle. Yet even here the recollections of spring and love are twice interrupted by a relapse into the world of wintry isolation. The poem strikes the reader as a faint echo of "Der Lindenbaum." This impression is brought about in part by the alternation of mood between sweet remembrances of spring and the frozen loneliness of the present moment.

Once again, as in "Rückblick," we find the use of bird imagery which encompasses both positive ("lustiges Vogelgeschrei") and negative ("Es schrieen die Raben. ...") associations. Between these extremes the roosters serve as traditional heralds of the dawn. Their shrill announcement of daybreak in stanzas two and five is perhaps influenced by the medieval *tageliet*.

Of particular interest in this poem is the picture of the ice-ferns ("Eisblumen") on the window panes.[11] This image is a peculiarly successful metaphor. It points to both spheres described in the poem. As "flowers" these formations partake of the world of spring, yet they are made of ice and as such are actually bound to winter. The theme of illusion is thus introduced through this image in a subtle way. It is furthermore particularly appropriate that they should appear at the window, which, as we have noted, is itself one of Müller's favorite ambivalent images, for it functions both to unite (through its transparency) and to separate two souls. The whole world of dream is thus pictorially represented in this delicate ice-fern image, and the principle of alternation between inside (dream) and outside (waking) worlds which is reflected in the alternation of stanzas in the poem crystallizes into the image of the window.

The poem progresses in a threefold pulsating rhythm: dream, waking, question / dream, waking, question. Stanzas one and two are inwardly related in that the dream of the beauties of nature is followed by an awakening of the eye ("Da ward mein Auge wach") and by an awareness of the prosaic world of wintry nature *outside*. Similarly, stanzas four and five are inwardly related—this time, however, on a different level. The dream is one of the raptures of love, and, correspondingly, it is this time not the eye, but the heart which awakens ("Da ward mein Herze wach") and ponders the world *within*. This polarity is not perhaps noticed at first but is eminently characteristic of Müller's *Erlebnisweise* and again is enhanced in this poem by the archetypal image of the window.

The relationship of the two stanzas which contain the questions (stanzas three and six) is also interesting. The first question, as we have seen, casts a bridge of metaphor between the realms of dream and waking. The second seeks to unite the two spheres on a higher plane (metaphorically: the ice-ferns will hopefully turn green), as an expression of the hope of reawakened love. Curiously enough, the last instance of the theme of hope expressed in a waking state within the cycle was also attached to the image of a leaf ("Letzte Hoffnung"). It is in keeping with the increasingly despairing mood of the cycle that this symbol now appears—not as a dried up *real* leaf clinging tenaciously to its branch, but as a real-unreal phantasmagoria of leafy patterns called forth by nature on a piece of glass. This distinction is in complete harmony with the state of consciousness which obtains in each poem. "Letzte Hoffnung" treats the theme of hope entirely in the waking state, whereas in "Frühlingstraum" the theme is enveloped in the imagery of dream.

The next two poems are best viewed together, for they complement one another in mood: utter dejection vs. defiant self-assertion. In "Einsamkeit" (p. 145) the motion is lethargic and dreary ("Mit trägem Fuß"). The poem's message is explained in the last two lines: "Als noch die Stürme tobten, / War ich so elend nicht." Indeed, the poem represents a psychological state somewhat more complicated than that in "Der stürmische Morgen," a state in keeping with the placement of the poem near the end of the cycle. In "Der stürmische Morgen" the wild tearings within the poet's breast found a direct correlative in the meteorological upheavals above his head. In the present poem, however, this one-to-one relationship is superseded by the acute sense of pain which gnaws mercilessly at the soul just by virtue of the absence of any sympathetic display in nature. The wanderer is thrust back entirely upon himself and the sense of isolation greatly increased.

In "Muth!" (p. 146) we have an entire poem which develops the theme of defiance of adversity, as this theme is introduced in "Der Lindenbaum" (stanza five). In both cases the young man strides ahead forcefully into the onslaught of wind and weather. In "Muth!" this defiance of nature is expanded upon through a conscious refusal to listen to the language of the heart which speaks of lost happiness. In "Der Lindenbaum" the wanderer closed his eyes in order to avoid seeing the tree, but was unable to avoid hearing its message. In "Muth!" the faculty of "inner hearing" is vigorously repressed: "Höre nicht, was er mir sagt, / Habe keine Ohren."

The three adverbs denoting inner happiness (stanza one: "hell," "munter"; stanza three: "lustig") are introduced in order to sustain artificially a mood which is no longer anchored in reality. For the true compass of the boy's disillusionment comes sharply into focus in the last two lines: "Will kein Gott auf Erden sein, / Sind wir selber Götter." The wanderer's despair, whose quality is very modern, has ultimately led him to a Promethean position. In the face of a sense of absurdity, and feeling himself abandoned by God, our wanderer's reaction is to raise himself to the status of a god. The self-assertive and defiant stand here expressed provides a powerful last gathering of forces before the collapse into utter alienation, as presented in the final poem. It is a titanic attempt to maintain a sense of identity out of nothingness. The obvious artificiality of this expansion of the "I," the fact that it lacks any deeper spiritual content, condemns it to deflation. The sheer nobility of this thoroughly honest, yet completely impossible "shot in the dark," gives to the poem its authentic ring.

One of Müller's most powerful poems, "Der Leiermann" (p. 146) presents a disturbing picture of the utter alienation of man. The themes of isolation and monotony introduced earlier in the cycle here reach their climax. The poem belongs at the end of the work by reason of this heightening of the cycle's central ingredients.

The organ-grinder is seen "hinterm Dorfe"—i.e., outside of the human community—an odd place for an organ-grinder with a little plate into which coins are generally dropped. But there are no coins, for, as K. G. Just has correctly observed, human beings no longer give one another anything.[12] This melancholy fact is substantiated by the circumstance that the organ-grinder's pathetic presence goes unnoticed by the ear and eye of man: "Keiner mag ihn hören, / Keiner sieht ihn an." The old man's fingers are numb and he is barely able to crank out a little music from his box ("Dreht er was er kann"). Even the music itself, that art so often praised as a link with the divine, has here fallen prey to monotony. It emanates automatically from a box, once the crank is propelled in a certain direction—a job just as well handled by an automaton. The mechanical nature of the "music" thus produced recalls instances of monotonous repetition of words earlier in the cycle (as for instance in "Das Wirthshaus": "Nur weiter denn, nur weiter").

The ultimate disconnectedness of man from the world is forcefully caught in the image of the barefoot man teetering on the ice. It is a picture of naked poverty which is even cut off from the necessary orientation to the earth's gravity ("Schwankt er hin und her"). It is not explicitly stated that the ice on which he stands is the covering of the river, but if it is, the "existential" dilemma is greatly deepened, as K. G. Just has observed, by the possibility that the thin layer of ice may at any moment give way and the old man disappear into the depths.[13]

The dogs, which howled before their masters' homes in "Gute Nacht" and drove the wanderer out of town with their barking in "Im Dorfe," now appear in an even more sinister form. They simply surround the old man and growl at him. The element of unpredictability involved gives to the situation a peculiarly eerie, dreamlike quality. The dogs no longer seem to belong anywhere and have become a bit of civilization reverted to primitivity.

In stanza four the indifference of the public is complemented by the indifference of the old man himself, who simply goes on turning the crank of his hurdy-gurdy in the very picture of meaninglessness. In the last stanza the wanderer addresses the old man. The dreary thought that he must identify himself with this pathetic individual is carried in a subtle manner by the epithet "wunderlich" ("Wunderlicher Alter"), an adjective earlier applied by the wanderer to the crow: "wunderliches Thier" ("Die Krähe"). The connection is deeper still. The archetypal image of the ring, which in its broken form pointed to broken love ("Auf dem Flusse") and in its closed form to a higher unity in death (the wreaths in "Das Wirthshaus"), also lies at the core of "Die Krähe" and "Der Leiermann." In the former, the crow describes ominous circles above the wanderer's head. The same monotonous rotating motion runs through the latter poem in the turning of the crank.

The wanderer's identification with the old man culminates in the question: "Willst zu meinen Liedern / Deine Leier drehn?" In this allusion to the songs of the cycle itself, the author injects an ironic comment on his own artistic production, and, in the larger sense, the world of poetry itself.[14] In so doing he identifies his own song-cycle with the meaningless world of the organ-grinder and, in a strikingly modern flourish, ironically "pulls the rug out" from the whole poetic undertaking.

In his discussion of "Der Leiermann," K. G. Just maintains that Müller has here come up against the "Grenzen des Sagbaren" and simultaneously the limits of what he as a lyric poet is able to master through language ("sprachlich zu bewältigen vermag").[15] We do not share this view for reasons which we shall set forth in the next two chapters. There is nevertheless no question but that "Der Leiermann" and, indeed, the cycle itself are a very successful and surprisingly "modern" poetic description of what it has become popular to refer to as "der unbehauste Mensch."

This cycle as a whole clearly lacks the inner plot development which gives "Die schöne Müllerin" its monodramatic character. "Die Winterreise" remains, as we have noted, more uniform in its structure, although there is a certain loose progression in the employment of themes. The cycle may well be compared to "Die schöne Müllerin" in one significant respect, however. It presents a succession of experiences and inner struggles which stand symbolically for a path through life. The cycle begins shortly after the ill-fated love affair—i.e., in a world of youthful enthusiasm thrown back upon itself by disappointment. It does not end in the wanderer's death, as do the "Müllerlieder," but with the related picture of old age. It is this compressing of a "path through life" (from youth to the inner experience of old age) into a series of characteristic psychological states which allows the cycle to symbolize the whole sweep of a particular destiny. It is a destiny permeated with suffering and pain. This has been keenly observed by Just, who aptly describes the whole as stations of a passion.[16] The stations focus upon the various inner struggles we have discussed: isolation, fond memories, hopes, death-wish, deception, dream, self-assertion, etc. The inherently musical quality of the poetic statement of this cycle is achieved through the repetition and interweaving of these themes, which occur, recur, and overlap in profusion. These elements are united in a loose thematic progression which moves from the hopes and disillusionments of youth to the resignation and paralysis of age. The wanderer's path proceeds against a background of shifting landscape which also shows the rough outlines of a progression. The journey begins with his trek out of town, moves along through the countryside, and gradually rises from the river valley into the snowy heights and gorges of the mountains ("Der Wegweiser," "Das Irrlicht"). From here it then slowly returns to the (or simply "a") village, which, however, is not entered. The final stage on the journey, death itself, is not described, but the mood is set and the associations are all established ("Das Wirthshaus"). Part of the power of the end of the cycle is derived form the tension resulting from the fact that the strong desire for death goes unfulfilled and the wanderer is condemned to continue an existence which has become meaningless and which must ultimately lead to the grave.

The picture of man's destiny, his "Weg" presented in this cycle, is radically different from that given in the "Müllerlieder." The difference finds its most vivid artistic expression in the central metaphor of the stream. In "Die schöne Müllerin" the wanderer is accompanied through life by the brook, and, finally, deaf to the latter's pleading ("Der Müller und der Bach") he simply gives up the struggle and "lets go," dissolving his being in the watery grave. In the "Winterreise" the opposite is true. Far from giving up the life struggle, this wanderer alienates himself more and more from the world by withdrawing into his own being and asserting this being with fierce determination. The concomitant soul-landscape can therefore no longer contain any rushing streams (except in memory), and it does not. They are all either frozen solid or dried up. The longed-for death which is not granted the miserable man asserts itself gradually, as a death of the soul, in the form of increasing alienation and despair. The danger of utter psychological isolation, of a freezing-up of the soul, gradually becomes stark reality and drives the wanderer into the contemplation of an old age devoid of any spiritual warmth and meaning whatever. This picture of old age is the logical outcome of an one-sided psychological state incapable of transcending the narrower limits of ego-centeredness.

The image of death which corresponds to the state of soul described above, will be quite the opposite of the gateway into the beyond portrayed in the "Müllerlieder" ("Und der Himmel da oben, wie ist er so weit!"). It must incorporate the qualities of non-transcendent, physically circumscribed experience characteristic of the cycle. This it does in the image of the physical grave. The two encounters with the ultimate question of death as treated in these cycles therefore contrast vividly with one another. The contrast comes most sharply into focus in the use of the metaphors of water vs. ice. In "Die schöne Müllerin" death is portrayed as a spiritual expansion (infinite tendency; metaphorically: water). In "Die Winterreise" it is viewed as a physical dead-end (finite tendency; metaphorically: ice). The latter state is—quite literally—a "point" of view which precludes any intimations of fulfillment or rebirth.

The question as to the extent to which "Die Winterreise" represents a personal "confession" of Wilhelm Müller will probably never be answered conclusively. There is insufficient biographical evidence to prove that Müller went through a crisis of these dimensions. On the contrary, the year 1821 brought the poet's marriage and his widespread fame as champion of Greek independence ("Griechenlieder"). He was an active and enthusiastic member of various "Liedertafeln" during the years in which the cycle was written, and virtually all the poems had been completed well before a series of upheavals which Müller, the school teacher, experienced in his clash with the headmaster. And he actually came out on top of that struggle. Müller was simply anything but inwardly alienated or depressed by the circumstances of life. He may, however, have been dimly conscious of his approaching death, and perhaps this subconscious awareness is the real voice which inspired such poems as "Die Krähe" or "Der Leiermann," which are obviously not contrived, but deeply felt. Five years after their composition he was dead. It is interesting to note that Franz Schubert struggled with this cycle while he himself was struggling with death, and the composition appeared only posthumously. We would thus not maintain that the poems of "Die Winterreise" represent the confession of an overwhelmingly tortured soul. On the other hand, they are not simply contrived. There speaks through them a great deal of inner suffering.

The living "stream" continued to rush along within the poet's soul, and in the year 1824 it broke forth out of the deepest wellsprings in the songs of the "Frühlingskranz." In the interim Müller wrote a great number of other poems (among them "Wanderlieder," "Devisen zu Bonbons," "Neue Lieder der Griechen," etc.) which are anything but the products of a psychological winter's night. We noted in the last chapter that the imagery of "Die Winterreise" is touched upon already in the "Müllerlieder" ("Die böse Farbe"). All of this evidence clearly points to the fact that Müller consistently had the inner experiences which have flowed into the "Winterreise" entirely under control. There can be no question of a protracted pessimism in the poet; yet these winter songs remain shattering. One senses that somehow Müller felt their frost in his own bones. The riddle of their inspiration may never be solved, but they will continue to arrest the attention of those who read or hear them by their vivid portrayal of a tragic destiny best characterized by the opening two lines of the cycle:

>Fremd bin ich eingezogen,
>Fremd zieh' ich wieder aus.

III

Frühlingskranz aus dem Plauenschen Grunde bei Dresden

From May 29 to June 13, 1824, the poet, then nearly thirty years old, spent perhaps the happiest days of his life as the guest of his friend, Count Friedrich von Kalckreuth, in the latter's summer residence Villa Grassi near Dresden. Walks through the blossoming spring landscape alternated with visits in Dresden, where Müller spent many hours with musicians, poets, and actors. On one occasion at a social gathering, some of Müller's drinking songs were so well received that the poet writes to his wife "Tieck hat sich den Bauch dabei gehalten..."[1] Among the most memorable musical events of those weeks were first a performance of *Der Freischütz* directed by Weber himself and also the latter's rendition of Haydn's *Seasons* on the first day of Whitsuntide.[2] The poet's reaction to the whole atmosphere of these days is summed up in a letter to his wife in the ecstatic words:

> Seit meinem Hiersein überbietet immer ein schöner Tag den andern; u heute am 2tn Pfingstfeiertage ist noch der schönste.[3]

The sheer joy of this period of rejuvenation has found expression in the "Frühlingskranz," whose poems Müller's friend and fellow poet Gustav Schwab considered among his finest. Schwab describes them as those "die nach meinem Urtheile als die lieblichsten und zugleich schwungreichsten

Produkte seiner Muse in unserer Sammlung glänzen."[4] It is remarkable that this collection should have been virtually ignored by scholarship.

It is somewhat difficult to speak of a "cycle" when describing this work. It is rather, as its name indicates, a "wreath"—one larger lyrical experience elucidated from various sides. The basic underlying theme is the triumph of the personified season, spring, over vanquished winter. The same dilemma confronts the critic in the case of this collection as in that of "Die schöne Müllerin." A number of very beautiful poems stand out against a background of charming but conventional and dated material. The point is thus not simply to reject the work *en masse* because of its trite passages but to sift out those poems which have lasting artistic merit and set them against the background of the whole, for purposes of clarification. Once again we shall undertake this somewhat delicate task, devoting particular attention to the better poems and passing quickly over the others.

The opening poem, "Frühlingseinzug" (p. 147), immediately presents the prerequisite to the encounter with spring: an open heart. This programmatic theme echoes as refrain through the entire poem: "Die Fenster auf, die Herzen auf! / Geschwinde! Geschwinde!" It binds together a stylized content—a medieval allegorical battle between spring and winter in which spring and his retinue of personified forces of nature emerge victorious. The image of the window, used so often by Müller to represent separation, is here employed as a metaphor for the human heart. The act of opening this "window" marks the transition from one season to another. The soul-landscape of winter is replaced by that of spring, and the forces of newly awakened life may stream into man's soul *provided* he makes room for them by opening the heart's "window". If he accomplishes this, the nightingale's song will resound within, as well as without: "Und horch, und horch, ein Wiederhall, / Ein Wiederhall aus meiner Brust!"[5]

The introduction of children into the scene ("Kinderfrühling," p. 148) is once again programmatic. As we shall see in the next chapter, the ability to perceive the delicate spiritual forces of renewal depends on an opening of the heart, and this process itself is dependent upon man's ability to restore within himself—his childhood.

The world of the "Winterreise" has now lost its grip on the soul: "Wilkommen, Lenz! Ich lebe noch / Und weiß von Leide nicht" ("Kinderlust," p. 149). In the seventh stanza of "Kinderlust" the religious dimension is introduced. Spring, personified as a young boy, scatters blessings over the land: "Nehmt, Kinder, nehmt! Es ist kein Traum! / Es kommt aus Gottes Haus." Spring, then, is in the service of God, spreading His gifts through the world. Significantly, it is the children who first recognize and accept these gifts.

We come now to one of Wilhelm Müller's most beautiful poems, "Die Brautnacht" (p. 150), in which a love-union of spring and earth is celebrated in an erotic-mystical image. This poem has also been completely neglected by scholarship. The polarity of masculine and feminine, spring and earth, which underlies the poem's content, is closely reflected in the details of its form. The four-beat iambic stanzas consist of alternating masculine and feminine lines with the corresponding rhyme scheme *a b a b* . The dynamism of the masculine lines is gently retarded in the feminine ones through the missing final accent. This unifying polar principle is relieved by the odd number of stanzas (7), which prevents the poem from freezing into a static form. A thematic similarity exists between this poem and one entitled "Himmel und Erde" (Hatfield, p. 386), which offers an interesting comparison but in no sense rivals the present poem for beauty.

The dramatically beautiful natural phenomenon of a spring storm is described in stanza one ("Es hat geflammt"). The immensity of the event is indicated through the references to time ("die ganze Nacht") and space ("am hohen Himmelsbogen"). Through the mood of tension a sense of expectation is invoked. This is relieved in stanza two as the entire phenomenon slowly comes into motion. This phenomenon, which gradually sinks downward from the vault of the heavens, is still viewed as entirely impersonal and is referred to by the pronoun "es" (line five). The sense of expectation now comes fully to expression: "Mit ahnungsvoller Schwüle." Thus the pure light-phenomenon is enriched first by motion and subsequently by a sensation of warmth. In line seven the acoustical impression is added: "Ein dumpfes Rollen zog daher." Through this process the shimmering light gradually is imbued with life. The entire complex descends from a super-terrestrial sphere, the atmosphere, and finally reveals itself to be a living being: "Und sprach von ferner Kühle." Through the metamorphosis of the dimly rumbling thunder into a voice, the majestic natural phenomenon discloses its identity as a stupendous living being which emanates from the dark background of the sky and descends amid darting bolts of lightning. The intensity of the mood of anticipation is enhanced by the contrasting words "Schwüle" and "Kühle," which express opposite sensory impressions that nevertheless combine with one another through the rhyme.

The tension is relieved as the warm raindrops, described as the tears of this living being, begin to fall. There now follows (lines eleven and twelve) the personification of the earth, which drinks in the rain. The mood of tension then attaches itself particularly to the earth itself, whose thirst is not quenched: "Die Erde trank, doch ungestillt / Blieb noch ihr heißes Sehnen." This union of the forces of the atmosphere and the being of the earth in a night filled with tension and anticipation is described in words which carry overtones at once erotic and mystical.

The turning-point in the poem has now been reached, and the fourth stanza describes the coming of morning. The relaxation of tension may now take place as the dawn ascends ("steigt empor"), and the poet breaks forth in this central stanza with the amazed question: "Welch Wunder ist geschehen?" Here in the middle of the poem he perceives the great transformation of the earth: "In ihrem vollen Blüthenflor / Seh' ich die Erde stehen." This image is, appropriately enough, described in static terms ("Seh' ich"), for the miracle has now taken place ("ist geschehen"), and the earth is spread out before the poet's eyes in its garment of bloom. This color-tableau is referred directly to the poet, to the lyrical

"I." It is the first and also the last time in the poem that the word "ich" occurs. Through its incorporation into the fourth and central stanza, in which the miracle of transformation lights up (quite literally, with the dawn) in the beholder's consciousness, the poet and reader are united with this wonder through a purely lyrical experience at the heart of the poem. The path from the impersonal "es" of the poem's beginning to the "ich" in the middle transmutes the contemplation of the miraculous outer phenomenon into an inner perspective which colors the last three stanzas with a mood of active wonderment. Each of these last three stanzas is introduced by a personal exclamation: "O Wunder, ... O still, ... O still." The symmetry of the poem's sevenfold construction is thus clear. Stanzas one to three form a unit as the outer phenomenon in nature is described in the third person. The last three stanzas (five through seven) are united through the active wonderment of the beholder expressed formally through the three exclamations. The poem's axis lies in the fourth and central stanza, which brings the advent of morning and introduces the first person singular pronoun ("ich"): the dawn without and the dawn within.

The question of stanza four ("Welch Wunder...") is transformed in stanza five into one of amazement: "O Wunder, wer hat das vollbracht?" This question is much more specific and seeks to know the nature of the being that has brought about the transformation. The question is then formulated pictorially through the description of the unfolding buds. Stanza five, line two ("Der Knospen spröde Hülle") in a sense incorporates all the feelings of anticipation of the first three stanzas in quintessential form through the image of a sheath of petals ("Hülle"). The question is now: "Wer brach sie auf in *einer* Nacht / Zu solcher Liebesfülle?" In one night all the expectations have found fulfillment. The juxtaposition of "Hülle" and "Fülle," opposites united through rhyme, echoes the earlier pair "Schwüle" and "Kühle" (stanza two). The short time span greatly heightens the mystery whereby in the image of the fragile buds the whole mood of expectation is transformed into one of fulfillment. The first line of the stanza is therefore particularly appropriate, for the human spirit can only properly approach any true miracle in a mood of reverent questioning. Intellectual explanations serve only to kill the aspect of wonder, and the poet can therefore really *only* pose a question, whereby he at the same time admires the wonder. German speaks accurately of such an admiration as "Be-wunder-ung."

In stanza six the exclamation of awe is transformed into a feeling of great intimacy, as the poet whispers "O still, o still" and focuses his attention upon the blushing of the flowers —expression of the earth's reaction to what has taken place. This employment of color gives expression to the mood of soul within the earth. It is interesting that Müller here introduces the verb "zittert" ("Ein rother Schauer zittert noch") which has the effect of a gentle echo of the tremblings of distant thunder and the flashing of lightning in the preceding night.

In the final stanza the mood of questioning is sustained as the question is referred to the active agent himself: "... und fragt den Bräutigam." The personification of nature and season now becomes manifest. Spring ("der Lenz") is the bridegroom and the earth ("die Erde") the bride. Through the convenient circumstance that in the German language the word for "spring" is masculine and that for "earth" feminine, these two nouns merge very neatly with "bridegroom" and "bride" ("der Bräutigam," "die Braut"), whereby the phenomenon of nature and the metaphorical, personified *being* in each case combine in an image held together by grammar.

The last line ("nach ihrer Hochzeitfeier") points back temporally even *beyond* the beginning of the poem. The "formal" marriage has thus taken place prior to the description beginning with the first stanza. In the poem itself, however, we experience the union of body and soul. This process generates in turn the mystical and religious mood which breathes through this interpenetration of the forces of nature.

An examination of the details of the poem's rhyme scheme is particularly rewarding. It is interesting to observe the use of consonants as they introduce the last accented syllable of each line. In the introductory stanzas the consonant is consistently dissimilar, as in "*N*acht" / "*P*racht," "*schw*er" / "*daʜ*er," etc. In the last two stanzas, however, we find the following pattern of consonants: "*d*och" / "*n*och," "*B*angen" / "*W*angen," "-*g*am" / "*k*am," "*F*reier" / "*F*eier." The consonants themselves have begun to move closer together, so that in these last stanzas their individual identity is preserved only through a slight difference in articulation.

An examination of the poem's vowel pattern reveals that whereas the use of rhyme in the middle of the poem is varied, beginning and end are joined by a strange similarity. The rhyme scheme of stanza one (*a o a o*) is echoed in reverse in stanza six: *o a o a* . We may then compare the patterns of the first and the last stanzas: *a o a o - a ei a ei* . Our attention is drawn at once to the *a*, which appears in both stanzas. If we now consider the word "Hochzeit" (stanza seven), the key word in the poem from the standpoint of content, we note that it is inwardly related to the rhyme pattern under discussion. This word, which points to the formal union of two individuals, contains the very two vowels which, in addition to the *a*, are contained in the first and last stanzas. Schematically the relationship may be depicted as follows:

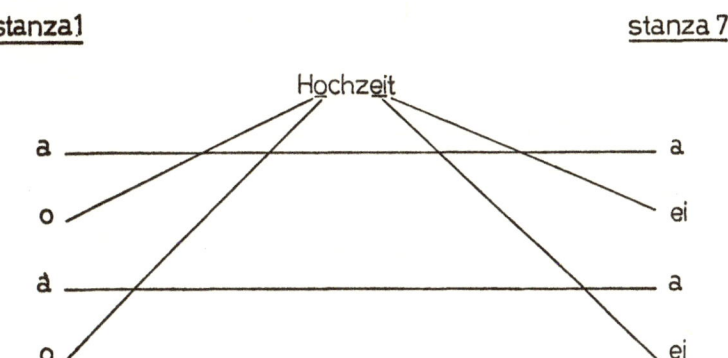

Into the first word of the last line of the poem, the line which contains the word "Hochzeit," there now creeps, interestingly enough, the vowel *a* . From the standpoint of our schema we can now say that the "formal" marriage celebrated in the poem echoes in the conjunction of the rhyme vowels *o* and *ei* (beginning and end of the poem) in the word "Hochzeit," while the all-embracing erotic-mystical union is reflected in the vowel *a* . The *a* is a dark, sonorous vowel, admirably suited to express this feeling. It appears as rhyme vowel in the first and last stanzas, and also at one other place in the poem—stanza five. Here it unites the two words "vollbracht" / "Nacht." Our schema must thus be expanded in order to encompass this second important rhyme phenomenon. We have purposely arranged the words "vollbracht" and "Nacht" in an unusual way in order that the nature of the phenomenon should be graphically illustrated. The mystical union of spring and earth in this night of love is thus reflected in the employment of the vowel *a*, whereas the formal union must always retain a double aspect and is reflected in the dissimilar vowels *o* and *ei*:

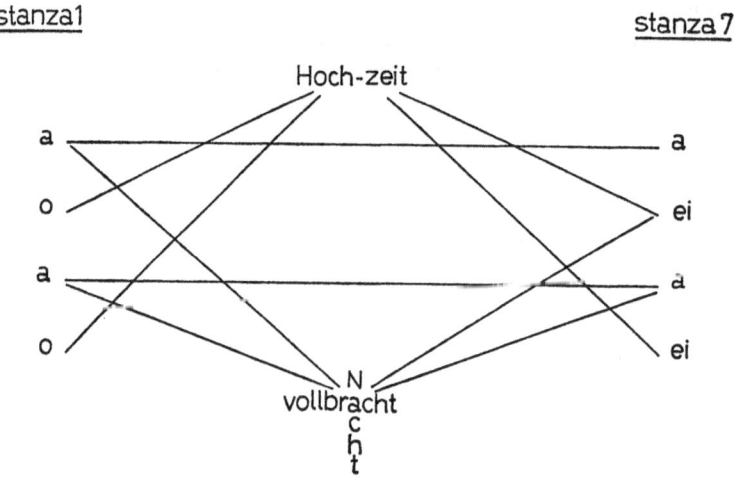

The progression of time in the poem begins in the past tense (stanza one), and straightway the phenomenon of nature begins to move (stanzas two and three). The present tense is reached in stanza four, the exact middle of the poem. Stanza five, also conceived in the present, points via a question back into the past. The attempt is here made to grasp something in the past from the vantage point of the present. This stanza hovers uncertainly as an answer is sought and leads over into stanza six, in which this hovering sensation takes on a visible, almost tactile form in the description of the bride: "Ein rother Schauer *zittert* noch / Um ihre frischen Wangen." (Italics mine.)

In the final stanza the double time-perspective is again introduced as we are admonished to direct the question to spring himself, "Der diese Nacht zur Erde kam / Nach ihrer Hochzeitfeier." It is important to note carefully all the dimensions of time in this stanza. It begins in the present, but the next to the last line points back to the past, when spring came to the earth. The surprise comes then in the last line—the thematic line continues over and beyond this past into an *earlier* past, at which time spring and the earth celebrated their marriage ("Hochzeitfeier"). This uncommon extension of the dimension of time back into an "ante-past" is the touchstone of a deeper appreciation of the poem, as we shall soon see.

In the two admonitions to the reader (line twenty-one: "merket doch," line twenty-five: "fragt den Bräutigam") the poet points gently toward the future, for the imperative mood implies an activity to be performed by someone. The questioning *stance* with which the poem ends directs our attention to a future in which we shall perhaps find the answers to our questions. The most important aspect of the use of time in the poem is however the progression from the past, through the present, which latter moment then directs our gaze back into the past—and then *beyond* this past into an even earlier moment. If we now keep in mind this inside-out aspect of the temporal development we may be in a position to gain a deeper appreciation of the poem's content.

The poem begins, as we have noted, with an impersonal image drawn from nature—an image which gradually takes on life and unites itself with another living being, the earth.

The natural phenomena and the metaphorical figures coincide: spring *is* the bridegroom and the earth *is* the bride. At the moment of their union in love the most personal sphere is reached ("Nacht" / "vollbracht"). This union is, however, also supported by the word "Hochzeit," which from the standpoint of rhyme casts a frame around the entire poem. However, this "Hochzeit" has taken place *prior* to the past time described at the poem's beginning. The living, *personal* union ("Hochzeit") was already an accomplished fact *before* the inanimate, *impersonal* union (the phenomena in nature). This insight hits us in a flash as we read the very last line in the poem. In what, then, does the deeper content of this insight actually consist? Ordinary phenomena of nature gradually disclose themselves to be living beings—indeed, human beings. These two beings consummate an erotic-mystical union, and the reader then hears of an earlier, formal marriage out of which the mystical union emerges like the blossom out of the bud. What then, is the unexpected insight? It consists in our sudden realization that something dead has become alive, and already *was* alive from the start! The mystical union which transpires pictorially and through the formal embodiment in rhyme is in itself remarkable. But the actual miracle, the "Wunder," inheres in the realization that we have experienced the mysterious metamorphosis of something dead into living beings—which were already present within the lifeless phenomena all along. The conclusion which we must draw is obvious: the "dead" phenomena are only appearances ("Schein"). That which at first appears inanimate gradually reveals itself to us in its true aspect: it is alive. In his naïve, rather instinctual way, Wilhelm Müller has drawn the inspiration for this poem out of the deeper wellsprings of the romantic world view.[6]

The argument might be raised that the contents of such a poem represent "only a metaphor" which has no validity in the "real" world. The answer to such an objection is obviously that it all depends upon the vantage point in thought, from which one draws a line between "appearances" and "reality." The *poem's* answer to such an objection must be that in the world of art that which our analytical intellect labels "appearance" is just as real as that which it arbitrarily isolates as true "reality." Indeed, the poem would be constrained to go one step further and point out that this "reality" is actually "dead" only in the eyes of the intellect, and that what the latter cheerfully assumes to be inanimate is in fact the *real* illusion, for it discloses itself to the more encompassing faculties of perception to be very much alive.

The all-pervading sense of joy which Müller felt during the weeks at the Count's residence near Dresden is incorporated into "Das Frühlingsmahl" (p. 151). This is another particularly beautiful poem which has been completely ignored by scholarship. The four-line folksong stanzas with alternating masculine and feminine rhymes lend the poem a formal balance, while the symmetry is once again relieved by the odd number of stanzas (seven).

We have observed that for Wilhelm Müller the deepest secrets of existence are approached through questions. The miller's lad, who senses an inner connection with the stream, searches by means of questions to find his way. "Die Winterreise" ends with the poet's question put to the old organ-grinder, and in "Die Brautnacht" the poet breaks out into questions filled with wonderment as he seeks to understand the transformation of the earth by spring. The pervasive sense of wonder in the face of the beauties of nature flows from the childlike quality of open-heartedness of which we have spoken and which is the prerequisite to the asking of the questions posed in "Das Frühlingsmahl."

The poem opens with a series of questions which all refer to the introductory word "Wer?" The poet seeks to know what higher being has spread out the beauteous landscape before him. This landscape is experienced as a metaphor for a banquet. In the first two stanzas the table is described which is to serve the host ("Wirth") for the spreading out of a meal. The white wildflowers surrounded by green foliage are the tablecloths. A high blue tent (the sky) is stretched over the whole, while the field is covered by a brightly-colored carpet, woven again out of wildflowers. A meal is being readied and the poet, filled with wonderment, asks who is the host.

As though the poet's question were superfluous, the answer presents itself at once in his soul (stanzas three and four). It is the host of Heaven and earth, whose storehouse is eternally filled. God's presence in the created world is not only immediately recognized; his voice is also heard by the poet. It is not necessary to seek out a specific phenomenon of nature (such as the wind) behind this voice. The call is perceived in an inner, spiritual way. God invites not only man, but all creatures ("was lebet und webet") to the great springtime feast. One is reminded of such a painting as Albrecht Dürer's "Maria mit den vielen Tieren,"[7] in which the Madonna is portrayed surrounded by all manner of animals. Here too one senses the underlying piety that shines through a scene in which all creatures of nature are touched and nourished by the spirit of God.

The imagery is enlarged upon in stanza five through the description of the blossoms of bush and tree. The flowers are described as "cups" ("Becher") from which sweet fragrances descend. From these cups all the creatures of nature (stanza six), and also man (stanza seven) are to drink. The Christian overtones are now clearly in evidence. The landscape is here experienced as a religious metaphor, as an embodiment of divine forces. We are reminded of the painting of P. O. Runge, in which nature is portrayed as filled with symbols corresponding to spiritual realities.

The mystical religiosity of this conception of the interweaving of the spiritual and natural worlds may seem at first glance totally unexpected. Yet the seeds of its formulation were planted roughly nine years earlier, when the twenty-one year old Müller was captivated by the personality of Louise Hensel, in Berlin. This girl's charming nature was enhanced by an intense piety which exerted a powerful influence over a number of young men, including Clemens Brentano.[8] Müller's passionate feelings for the girl were anchored (as are those of the miller's lad in "Die schöne Müllerin") more in wishful thinking than in reality. Nevertheless, the religiosity of her world left a strong imprint on him, as his diary shows. We find for instance the following entry dated December 24th, 1815:

> Ich hatte nehmlich heute Abend mich zum Genuß des heiligen Abendmahls vorbereitet. Der alte Hermes hatte seine Hand auf mein Haupt gelegt u gesagt: Deine Sünden sind dir vergeben. Auch ich selbst hatte mich durch brünstiges Gebet vorbereitet.[9]

During this period (1815-1817) Müller's attention had been drawn to the writings of Novalis and Jakob Boehme. The absorption of the world view of these writers cannot help but have complemented and deepened his love for the world of folk poetry in *Des Knaben Wunderhorn*, which he also studied at the time. A very interesting passage in the diary discloses Müller's intense personal reaction to Novalis:

> Ich habe in diesen Tagen viel in Novalis gelesen, der mich oft gar wunderlich ergriff, es schien die Stimme desselben nicht von außen zu mir hereinzuklingen, sondern aus mir hervor. Es schien mir, als hätte ich das Alles schon lange sagen wollen, wäre aber stumm gewesen.[10]

Such intense feelings for the ideas of a Novalis or a Boehme of course do not express themselves outwardly in the following years through the various activities and writings of a young man who was also an intellectual, urbane *Weltkind*, busy with the affairs of the outer world. Yet neither are they lost. They continue to develop and are drawn upon later in life. In the year 1824 these feelings were reawakened when near Dresden the beauties of nature met something within the poet's soul—perhaps a dim sensing of his death three years hence— which enabled him to look out into nature with a new spiritual sensitivity.

In the language of this poem, the disparity of nature and

spirit, of outer and inner, is overcome, as the soul-landscape, through the deepened use of metaphor, becomes a vehicle for the intimation of a spiritual, a sacramental act. The imagery is *not* handled in an obvious, one-to-one allegorical fashion, and it is therefore wrong to force it into a clear-cut pattern of religious symbolism. Yet this symbolism is present in the most delicate *reflection*, particularly in the image of the blossoms as cups from which the creatures and man are to drink. There is a gentle allusion to the archetypal Cup of the Last Supper. Just as in terms of traditional theology man experiences in the wine of the sacrament the blood of the Lord, so does he here, in concert with all the creatures of the earth, draw spiritual nourishment from the cups of the flowers which the divine Host has placed in the landscape. We have often had occasion to speak of the latter as the "soul-landscape" of the "lyrical I." In the present poem it is again viewed as such, with one crucial addition. The personal world of soul, metaphorically expressed through images with pleasurable or painful associations, is here heightened and serves as a vehicle for the poetic elaboration of a superpersonal, entirely spiritual act, which weaves between the earthly and the heavenly spheres. In keeping with the Romantic writers' view of nature, God is here seen as livingly present in the landscape, where He passes out His gifts. The whole conception of this deed (table, cloths, cups) is one of a sacramental communion of an unorthodox and mystical kind between God and His creatures, in *nature*. As such it cannot be conceived of in literal terms, but only metaphorically, in terms of the awakened spiritual eye of the poet who in the best Romantic tradition senses the "correspondences" between the world of nature and that of the spirit, and learns to read in them and participate in their regenerative force.

We will recall that in "Die schöne Müllerin" the extended monologue is broken through in the last two poems by the introduction of the speaking voice of the stream. This awakening of the inner ear ("Der Müller und der Bach") was made possible by the shock within the soul, occasioned by disappointment. Similarly, in "Das Frühlingsmahl" the poet's mood of wonder at the beauties of the created world awakens in him a new inner hearing (stanza six). The voice of God now becomes audible, and the indirect call of line fifteen ("Und ruft was lebet und webet") is transformed into direct speech ("Heran, was kriecht und fliegt," etc.). Through this motif of the awakening of a higher faculty of hearing, a new ability to listen to the divine spoken word imparts to the poem a distinct feeling of the Whitsun season (in which it was written) which finds direct expression in the next to the last poem of this collection ("Pfingsten").

The voice of God invites all the creatures to the banquet table and, in the last stanza, addresses man himself, who in keeping with the usual Christian tradition, is referred to as a pilgrim to Heaven. Just a touch of the Dionysian is contained in the phrase "Hier trinke trunken dich."[11] This concept represents a purification of a notion treated in the very much less spiritual "Trinklieder," in which the intoxication of "spirits" is seen as a path back into paradise.[12]

Having drunk the draught proffered by God, man is admonished to sink down upon his knees and direct his attention to the Host Himself: "Und sinke selig nieder / Auf's Knie und denk' an mich!" Man is asked to pray, and the prayer consists in a meditative focusing of thought upon the Being Who is speaking. The entire content of the poem must be understood in this inward sense. The flower-cups do not literally contain wine. They are divine symbols, ciphers which must be properly read by the awakened soul. Through a heightening of the faculties of sight, hearing, feeling and meditative thought ("... denk' an mich!") the poet actively experiences the outer landscape in a purely spiritual, symbolic sense as a sacramental banquet. In so doing he answers to the wish of God and finds nourishment for the soul.

In the course of the poem man has exchanged the role of speaker with God. This is ultimately made possible by the childlike quality of wonder and awe which from the first enables the poet to ask the key question ("Wer hat ...?"), rather than to jump at once into detached commentary upon the scene before him. Through this childlike quality of soul the inner ear is awakened, and he finds himself the recipient of the freely bestowed gift of understanding. Thus the poem is framed-in by two pronouns which contain in quintessential form this very relationship between man and God. The first word in the poem is a question, posed by man ("Wer ...?") and the last word in the poem is an answer, spoken by God ("mich!").

In the poem "Erlösung" (p. 152) the eye of the poet returns to an image familiar to us from the previous chapter: the frozen river. A process of liberation is set in motion as the warm spring sunlight thaws the ice covering and is felt by the fish underneath. This image serves as a simile for the release of pent-up feeling and the resultant awakening of the faculty of sight in man. Once again, the element of warming light which operates materially in the melting of the river's ice, is metaphorically imbued with spiritual substance in the second half of the poem, when the awakening of the poet's heart and eye are described.

The poem's formal structure is of peculiar interest. The first half of the poem depicts a landscape almost lifted bodily out of "Die Winterreise." The second half portrays a scene completely characteristic of the "Frühlingskranz." The syntax itself carries the process of transformation at work in the poem. The syntactical fulcrum is the central independent clause: "Fühlet meine Brust sich frei" (stanza two, line two). Just as the rising water frees itself from the icy cover of a river this clause gradually peels its way out of the preceding dependent clauses, quite literally "wie aus Kerkerqual." This line "Fühlet meine Brust sich frei" fulfills thematically the promise of the poem's title—the feelings of man are liberated by the active, personified warmth of spring's sunlight ("des jungen Lebens Gluth"). Interestingly enough, the syntax now proceeds in a manner which balances out the first half of the poem. The key line is followed immediately by another dependent clause introduced by "Wenn." The two clauses of the last stanza, both introduced by "Und," are arranged in apposition to the "wenn"-clause—that is they are in a sense dependent upon a dependent clause. The effect of this complicated syntactical structure in the poem is to focus attention upon the central moment of release which is prepared slowly ("under the surface") and carries with it, after having burst forth, a series of consequences (syntactically: a series of dependent clauses; thematically: a progressive expansion of the visual perspective through the clouds, the heavens, the ether).

The parallel use of metaphor is clear. The winter is for the soul of man what the ice is for the river and its fish: a prison. The ray of sun which thaws the river's ice also tears apart the tent of clouds and reveals the sphere of the heavens beyond ("Und das Dach ist abgedeckt, / Das mich von dem Himmel schied"). The clouds which in "Die Winterreise" represent turmoil in the landscape of the soul (Cf. "Der stürmische Morgen") are here parted by a force of light and warmth which streams in *from without* and which frees the soul from its imprisonment. The dynamic sweep of this event is subtly indicated by the change of verbs. The verb used to describe the sun's penetration of the river's ice is "dringt," whereas its sundering of the clouds is rendered by the verb "reißt." This enhances the sense of innate vitality already attached to the spring sun through the phrase "des jungen Lebens Gluth."

Once the cloud cover has been parted, man's vision is no longer separated from the sky above. The German noun "der Himmel" has of course the added meaning "Heaven," which renders more explicit the implied mood of religious awakening in the poem. Man's power of sight is expanded, and his eye is said to see "durch den Äther." The underlying religious associations enable us to see that Müller's description of the awakening of the eye must be understood in more than physical terms. The eye as a bodily organ remains passive; indeed, it is in a sense entirely "selfless" and merely allows for the entry of light, color, and imagery into the consciousness of man. Its "awakening" can be conceived of only in spiritual terms, as it clearly is in this poem. Once awakened it is able to extend its range into the "ether," the "Himmel."

We recall the last poem of the "Winterreise," "Der Leiermann," in which the mood of alienation had become so intense as to paralyze both the ear and the eye of man, even in the face of abject misery: "Keiner mag ihn hören, / Keiner sieht ihn an." In the "Frühlingskranz" both of these crucial organs of perception are reanimated. The role played in the poem "Das Frühlingsmahl" by the awakening of the faculty of hearing is complemented in "Erlösung" by a similar awakening of the faculty of sight. The opening of a spiritual "inner ear" is here followed by the opening of an "inner eye" which comes to life behind the activity of the bodily eye. It would perhaps be tempting to see in the image of the fish a reflection of ancient Christian symbolism in the poem. We feel that it is quite impossible to speak of any conscious employment of such a symbol here. And, moreover, to do so is unnecessary. A sensitive reader will be fully aware of the— however unorthodox and mystical—Christian *atmosphere* which pervades this whole "Frühlingskranz," from the role of the child to the imagery of a sacramental meal. The awakening of a higher sense of hearing itself suggests the mood of Whitsuntide reflected in the next to the last poem's title. Furthermore, it is itself the season in which the poems were written. The present poem may contain no specifically Christian symbols. Its unique gift within the collection is in keeping with this mood, however, through its portrayal of the awakening of the eye of man from the darkness of winter by the inpouring of light and warmth.

In "Der Peripatetiker" (p. 153) an entire allegory is developed out of the image of spring as a wandering scholar-teacher. The dead black letters of ordinary books are contrasted with this teacher's "living texts," the flowers that cover mountain and vale.[13] The teacher in this "Wanderschule" is termed "der Weise aller Weisen," yet he seems to act as if all were a joke (stanza six). Here we see Müller's tendency to combine the themes of wisdom and wit, of deep knowledge of life and the levity of humor. This combination of naïveté and intellect lies behind his love for epigrammatic utterances. A characteristic one which combines in somewhat more classical terms this curious mixture of the theme of learning and the relief of humor is epigram number I/72:

"Was er weiß, macht ihn heiß"
Viele lange Jahr' es währt,
Daß ein Tag den andern lehrt.
Wird der jüngste Tag zu heiß,
Ist's von Allem was er weiß.
(Hatfield, p. 318)

In the traditional "book of nature" the flowers represent letters, whereas in the final poem of this cycle, "Xenion," and in "Ein ungereimtes Lied" (Hatfield, p. 153) they stand for poems. The poet's admonition: "Lest, o lest die lieben Schriften" (stanza eight) turns on the double meaning of the German "lesen"—"to read" and "to gather up." Because these letters are alive, in contrast to the black letters of printed books, the man who reads them will feel love for their author (stanza eight). The true identity of the spirit which speaks through this experience in nature is linked to the word "Wahrheit" (stanza eight). We shall return to this when we examine the poem "Xenion."

The image of the fish which felt the warmth of spring's sun in "Erlösung" serves as the central motif in "Die Forelle" (p. 154) in which the creature's carefree and happy existence is presented as an example for man. The poem's tendency is thus basically didactic: "... sei meine Lehrerin." The conception of the brook as a metaphor for the onrushing stream of destiny ("Die schöne Müllerin") is touched upon in this poem. The trout swims up over the rocks "Grad', als wäre das ihr Weg!" (stanza two), an image which in the last stanza is applied to the poet's own life. He asks the trout to teach him the technique of handling life's challenges: "Über Klippen weg zu hüpfen, / Durch des Lebens Drang zu schlüpfen."

The poem is devoid of trite or Anacreontic embellishments and, despite its simple theme, possesses a real charm. This lies in no small measure in the delightful leaping rhythm of the lines. The beat is trochaic, a meter which imitates the falling motion of the water. Yet the sprightly spring of the imagery gives the reader the decided impression that he really ought to be reading iambs. This is even underscored by the burden of grammar in such a sentence as stanza one, line five, in which the first accented syllable is a complete word, set off from the following by a comma: "Sucht, gelockt von lichten Scheinen." In this line the trochaic scanning demands the very unorganic foot: "Súcht, ge-..." Any sensitive reader will prefer to separate these two units and attach the prefix "ge-" to its verb. He will then read the word as an iamb and proceed with the rest of the line on the same basis:

_ / ᴜ _/ ᴜ _/ ᴜ _ / ᴜ
"Sucht, gelockt von lichten Scheinen."
Exactly the same thing may be maintained in the case of such lines as stanza two, line four:

_ / ᴜ _/ᴜ _/ ᴜ _
"Grad', als wäre das ihr Weg!" and stanza three, line six:

_ / ᴜ _/ ᴜ _/ ᴜ _/ ᴜ
"Nicht, ob sie es soll ertragen."

The result is the repeated sense of a forward thrust which keeps playing *against* the trochaic meter. This tension, created by Müller's characteristically sensitive use of rhythm, brings vividly alive the feeling of sprightly hopping associated with the fish and longed for by the poet himself: "Lehre mir den leichten Sinn, / Über Klippen weg zu hüpfen,..."

The next poem of particular interest is "Pfingsten" (p. 156), a hymn in free verse to the spirit of God. It expresses programmatically the mood of reverent awe which we have encountered already in this cycle. It is rooted in the Klopstock tradition, yet shows characteristic signs of Müller's poetic imagination.

The exclamation "O heilige Frühlingswonne" with which the poem opens is directed not at a mythologized phenomenon of nature but to the spirit itself which fills nature in the spring season. In lines two through seven the poet describes in exalted language the powerful descent of this spirit from distant reaches down into the world: "Strahlend und flimmernd / In himmlischen Schauern." The Whitsun spirit approaches the earth through mountains and valleys until it finally enters the breast of man (line seven). This cosmic contraction of spiritual forces from the infinite periphery into the circumscribed space of the human breast is reflected not only in this opening image of the first seven lines but also in the entire poem.

In the following lines the spirit which man now experiences inwardly is recognized and named: "Ja, du bist es, Geist Gottes." The poet here answers the phenomenon by describing it: "Du gießest dich aus / über die Welt." The general feeling of awe is hereby transformed into a conscious recognition which throws the poet back upon himself. Once he has in this sense awakened to the phenomenon, he is faced with the question of how to respond. Thus in the middle of the hymn there are two questions, posed by man and directed to himself. He first asks: "Soll ich auf die sonnige Höhe steigen / Und beten?" and then: "Soll ich in dem dunklen Thale liegen / Und sinnen?" The first question reflects the poem's opening situation – the reverent gaze of man directed into the outward infinity of space. The second reflects the polar opposite, inner sphere which hearkens back to the entry of the spirit into the human breast. Once again we notice that Wilhelm Müller approaches an intellectually unfathomable mystery through questions.

In the second half of the poem the poet addresses himself to his own responsibility for the preservation of life. His desire not to harm even the worm and the mosquito testifies to the entrance of the cosmic spirit into his soul. Through his self-questioning he finds himself led to increasingly finite spheres until finally he recognizes in the most minute creatures the same spirit which he had previously seen in the widths of space. This spatial progression from limitless expansion to extreme contraction is rendered doubly powerful through the image of the mosquito, itself almost invisible in its tenuous, aerial existence. The transformation is also carried by the repetition of the light-imagery (line three: "strahlend," line twenty-four: "Strahl"). This treatment of the element of light metamorphoses the spirituality of the Whitsun season from cosmic space into the immediate environment of earth's creatures. The mosquito is actually portrayed as though held in the light-filled atmosphere. The poet has here successfully portrayed a mood of wonderment in the face not only of cosmic grandeur but also of the humblest creatures of nature.

The formal structure of the poem is eminently characteristic of Wilhelm Müller's mode of thought. Despite the flood of free verse and the hymnic language, a dividing-line is drawn which separates the poem's content into two poles. The result is an almost architectural sense of balance which appears in the polarity of beginning and end, and also in the two questions which themselves once again reflect the upper and lower spheres in nature.

The polarity in the poem is transcended by a higher unity which is effected through the progressive development of the contents. In "Erlösung" the warm sunlight falls through the ice, causes it to melt and brings new life to the fish underneath. In "Pfingsten" the spirit of Whitsuntide pours from above down into the breast of man, who through his conscious recognition of its presence is enabled to sense it also in the creatures about him and thereby through an inner enlightenment feel reverence for their existence.

The Greek title of the final poem, "Xenion" (p. 156), means "gift to a guest." The poem is an expression of thanks to Count von Kalckreuth, in whose summer residence Müller had spent several weeks. To him Müller here dedicates the poems of the "Frühlingskranz": "Und die neuesten sind dein."

The poem is of interest in its connection with the theme of poetry itself. The poet's muse is here personified and wanders through the countryside singing her songs. Just as in "Der Peripatetiker," spring scatters his floral gifts which must be gathered in ("read") by the muse: "Meine Muse suchte Lieder, / Wenn sie Maienblumen las." We may now ask ourselves who it is that Müller has in mind when he describes the workings of the spirit of spring in this way. In "Der Peripatetiker" he is termed "der Weise aller Weisen," and his texts are said to be "voller Wahrheit." The poem "Xenion" stands immediately after "Pfingsten" in the collection. Müller is here pointing in a restrained way to the Holy Spirit, the

Spirit of the Whitsun festival. A further light is thrown upon this fact in the poem "Sonntag" (Hatfield, pp. 388-389). In this poem the angels speak a threefold prayer which is directed to the Father (stanzas four to six), the Son (stanza seven), and, finally, the Holy Spirit (stanza eight). The latter is referred to by the angels as "Geist der Wahrheit." Ultimately, this is for Müller the Spirit Who, during the Whitsun season, bestows gifts upon the poet's soul and provides the inspiration for his song.

In Wilhelm Müller's total lyrical production there are three collections of songs which deal, each in its own way, with the struggles and victories of an individual human soul. These are "Die schöne Müllerin," "Die Winterreise," and "Frühlingskranz." The first two cycles are each felt to be unified statements, first by virtue of their thematic contents ("plots"), and, secondly, through the characteristic danger to the psychological equilibrium of the lyrical "I," which comes to expression in a different manner in each cycle. These characteristic dangers (which center ultimately upon the theme of death, physical and spiritual) play no significant role in Müller's other song-cycles. For this reason, these other cycles, interesting as they are in limited ways, fall short of the unified artistic statements of those we have discussed. One need only think of the "Muscheln von der Insel Rügen," drawn from the observation of the life of the "Volk," or the "Griechenlieder," which celebrate the cause of freedom in the political sphere.[14] The poems of such cycles as these touch only fleetingly upon the deeper questions of the inner balance of the soul (cf. "Vineta"). Their contents are thematically circumscribed (folkways, political freedom). The same is also true of the other collections, including the group "Johannes und Esther," which revolves about the narrower religious question of the conversion of a Jewish girl to Christianity. Only in the "Frühlingskranz" do we once again find a series of poems which may be compared to the first two cycles we have interpreted. It rests upon the much broader basis of the purely lyrical encounter with nature and treats of the poet's own inner experiences. In this cycle the psychological realm is expanded and enriched by themes of an objective spiritual nature which transcend the narrower confines of the ego. For this specific reason we feel that it is justified to see in this collection an impulse which complements the other two cycles and, in a sense, overcomes the one-sidedness of each. This it accomplishes in a body of imagery which is *not* thematically narrow in scope as is that of the remainder of Müller's cycles.

The step taken by the "Frühlingskranz" beyond the thematics of the other two collections we have discussed is fundamental. The "Müllerlieder" and the "Winterreise" are the only song-cycles in which our childlike poet so clearly describes the dangers to which the naïve soul of a romantic "wanderer" (and that of course means the soul of "man") is exposed. In each case a specific struggle takes place in the psychological realm. In the "Frühlingskranz," on the other hand, the individual is portrayed in the contemplation of nature. The stance is not one of the assertion of personal will but of the opposite state—the active *receiving* of nature's message through awakened faculties of hearing and sight. This inner bearing of harmonious rest, sought in vain by the wanderer in each of the other cycles, provides the condition whereby the individual experience is enabled to transcend the purely psychological domain and unite itself consciously with the spiritual. An individual posture is thereby presented which provides the deepest answer which Müller found to the very real dangers which he portrayed in the other two collections. This answer does not spring from the enthusiasm for a *cause célèbre* ("Griechenlieder"), an interesting problem of religious allegiance ("Johannes und Esther"), or fascination with folkways ("Muscheln") but rather from the timeless theme of the individual's selfless encounter with nature and God.

If we recall to mind the central metaphor which gave imaginative expression to the soul's endangerment in each of the other cycles, we shall see that in this sphere, also, the "Frühlingskranz" relieves the tensions created by their one-sidedness. In the "Müllerin" the death of the soul was linked to the metaphor of water (flight into the beyond; formlessness), in the "Winterreise" to that of ice (isolation in the grip of ego-centeredness; dead, frozen form). In the "Frühlingskranz" the lyrical "I" has attained an inner balance and stands in a soul-landscape of blossoming life, in a world of *living form*. Only here does this "I" truly find itself. Through the very absence of a preoccupation with self-interest, a psychological "middle position" is found which is capable of spiritual growth. The outer *and* inner eye comes alive, "Welches durch den Äther sieht." The Whitsun spirit is able to pour itself "strahlend und flimmernd" into the soul, and the latter is thereby transformed and imbued with reverence for life. Müller obviously did *not* consciously set about to provide an answer to the tragedies of "Die schöne Müllerin" and "Die Winterreise" by writing the "Frühlingskranz." To believe that he had done so would be to read into his mind a conscious plan which was clearly not there. He wrote the "Frühlingskranz" because of the sheer innate joy he experienced at that time and place in his short life. The fact that these poems *do* represent an answer—and the most profound answer that Müller ever found—to the archetypal problems of the other two cycles is something which we find wonderful indeed.

At first reading it is possible that one could arrive at the opinion that in the "Frühlingskranz" Müller gives himself over to an uncontoured wave of emotional intoxication. A careful reading, however, will show that this view is erroneous. Despite an occasional phrase, such as "Hier trinke trunken dich" ("Das Frühlingsmahl"), the poet's consciousness remains consistently in clear focus. In fact, the very poem which from the point of view of its content harbors the greatest danger of dissolution ("Pfingsten") reveals in the precise architecture of its construction a crystalline clarity of form. There is here not the slightest trace of a mystical "Rausch" or lack of control on the part of the author. Childlike reverence and a sober sense of form are two of the basic forces at work in Wilhelm Müller's poetic imagination, and they both come clearly to expression in "Pfingsten."

Müller's tendency to feel his way to a religious experience by starting from the concrete physical environment is a characteristic of his innermost disposition and is rooted in his sense of polarity. He was of the opinion that the material world was finally meaningful only when its spiritual counterpart was not forgotten. But at the same time he felt that the spiritual is rendered meaningful to man as he relates it to his experiences in the physical world. This stance is inherent in many of his lyrical poems, but has once again crystallized into conceptual terms in an epigram:

"Form und Geist"

Kannst du ohne Erdenbild himmlischen Verstand
    verstehen,
Wirst du ohn' Gefäß den Wein keltern, gähren,
    trinken sehen.
(No. I/43. Hatfield, p. 313)

The religious inspiration which the "wanderer," the poet, the "lyrical I" of any man can experience in the transformation of the soul-landscape of winter into that of spring is not attained merely intellectually. The human being must find his way inwardly to what we might best term, paradoxically, the "maturity of childhood." He accomplishes this through the development of a new organ of cognition. This organ is the human heart, which he must "open" in order that spiritual light and warmth may enter. It is this mystery to which Müller points with cheerful naïveté in the opening lines of his "Frühlingskranz":

Die Fenster auf, die Herzen auf!
Geschwinde! Geschwinde!

IV

Wilhelm Müller's Poetic Imagination

One of the central tasks confronting the interpreter of any literary work is to discriminate between the body of traditional themes, motifs, and metaphors from which the poet draws his material and the unique functions of creative imagination whereby he impresses upon this material the stamp of his individuality. To neglect either factor means ultimately to present a one-sided picture of the author's work.

In the case of a poet such as Wilhelm Müller, who obviously cannot vie with the prominent writers of the genre but is—so we hope to have shown—more than an imitator, the whole question of uniqueness is particularly difficult to deal with. This difficulty results from the fact that the song-cycles are encumbered with a good deal of conventional "baggage" which today appears so blatantly dated as to attract immediate attention to itself, to the decided detriment of the more significant and personal statement. Indeed, in the case of Müller the latter has long been assumed not even to exist, so submerged has it seemed by the trivialities with which it is clearly encrusted. We hope to have shown that it is possible in the case of this poet to penetrate the underbrush of convention and cliché and be pleasantly surprised to uncover a number of poems of some considerable beauty and depth. In so doing we have undertaken to identify and to describe the uniqueness of content and form in each of them in an exact way. This has led us to discover a substratum of content and particularly of metaphor and *Erlebnisweise* which runs through the works and shows itself to be typical of this particular poet's creative imagination. This then gives us the specific means whereby to form a picture of his uniqueness, the "temper" of mind and heart which are his alone.

In this final chapter we shall undertake to penetrate a little deeper into the specific workings of Müller's mode of experiencing the world as this finds expression in the form and content of his lyrical poems. The whole job is particularly fascinating because of the deceptively naïve, unassuming air of the poems, which at first hardly seems to invite more careful analysis. But the man was obviously not as simple-minded as one might be led to assume. His intense scholarly and intellectual activity belies this notion. And the poems themselves, particularly those to which we have devoted especial attention, speak quite another language. We shall therefore now point once again to the characteristic imagery and mode of experience underlying Müller's perception of the world and hereby draw a larger picture of his active imagination. This imaginative realm is the limitless sphere of consciousness itself, out of which the elements of a poet's statement arise.

Polarity and Balance

We have repeatedly noted Müller's inclination to view a phenomenon as a polarity ("Freud' und Leid," the color green, etc.) which is then seen on a higher level as a unity. A very interesting poem which appeared posthumously, "Selbstbeschauung" (Hatfield, pp. 429-430), presents a polarity which develops gradually out of a unified vision:

"Selbstbeschauung"

    Haben ausgetobt die Stürme,
    Sind verhallt die Donner,
    Sind verglüht die Blitze,
    Siehe, da hebet aus Nebeln und Wolken

>   Klar der Mond sein großes Auge
>   Und beschauet im Spiegel des Meeres
>   Sich und den Himmel.
>
>   Seele des Menschen, du gleichest dem Monde!
>   Aus den tobenden Stürmen der Brust,
>   Aus der irdischen Freuden und Leiden
>   Donnernden, blitzenden Ungewittern,
>   Aus des Wahnes Nebelschleiern,
>   Aus der Sünde Wolkennacht,
>   Hebst du verklärt und geläutert
>   Dein ewiges Auge
>   Und beschauest im Spiegel des Himmels
>   Dich und die Erde.

As in "Des Baches Wiegenlied," the phenomenon of death is described in the metaphor of a rising moon. Both the moon (stanza one) and the human soul (stanza two) are pictured as an eye. The direction of the eye's gaze is however the opposite in each case. The moon "... beschauet im Spiegel des Meeres / Sich und den Himmel." The poet then addresses the human soul, saying "Du... beschauest im Spiegel des Himmels / Dich und die Erde." From the standpoint of the moon, the reflecting surface is that of the ocean upon the earth. To the moon, the heavens appear as something outward which is also reflected in the ocean. The moon's gaze is directed downward, toward the other heavenly body. From the standpoint of the human soul, however, the reflecting surface is the heavens themselves. To the soul, the earth (i.e., the single "heavenly body") appears as something outward which is reflected in the mirror of the heavens. Just as the moon's gaze is directed downward, so also is that of the soul directed upward into the infinity of the heavens.

Here we once again have a polarity of experience, a polarity which develops organically out of a use of parallel imagery. The resultant polarity is however transcended metaphorically on a higher level. The image of the ocean as a watery mirror is expanded until it covers the vast extent of the sky. The sky is itself a mirror and, simply as *image*, coincides naturally with that of the ocean. This "Himmel" is (1) in the concrete sense, a conglomerate of numberless heavenly bodies; (2) in the imaginative sense, a watery ocean of infinity; and (3) in the deepest metaphorical sense, a mystical-religious element in which the soul experiences itself and the earth reflected, as in a divine mirror. Here Müller takes his starting-point as usual in the image of a phenomenon of nature, elevates this into the realm of myth, and then proceeeds thereby to portray the moment of death in a powerful mystical vision which overcomes the polarity of the earthly and heavenly reflections through the metaphor of water. This whole process is eminently characteristic of Wilhelm Müller's mode of experiencing, and gives expression to his intuitive conception of deeper riddles of existence in imagery of cosmic beauty.

It was Müller's unusually flexible *Erlebnisweise* which enabled him, in his better poems, to transcend his own apparent limitations. He was equally at home as a critic and editor as he was as a lyric poet. The intellectual bent of his mind leads repeatedly to succinct statements which contain the typical polarity of which we have been speaking. The polarity may in this case result from a juggling of words, as in the following epigram:

"Rath und That"

Wer jeder That sich unterfängt, der kömmt zu
  keinem Rath;
Wer jeden Rath berathen will, der kömmt zu
  keiner That.

(III/62, Hatfield, p. 359)

Through the epigram's paradoxical ring the reader senses that a resolution of these opposites may be possible on a higher level. Similar processes are described in such epigrams as "Weinen und Lachen" (III/67, p. 359) or "Die helle Stirn," and "Die finstere Stirn" (II/21, 22, p. 326). The absence of any higher resolution of the extremes within the epigrams themselves is not difficult to explain. The epigram is the most intellectual form of poetry one can imagine. In this form a conflict can be chiselled out in precise terms. The third sphere, however, in which the opposite poles are reconciled, is qualitatively distinct from the intellectual thought structure in which the problem is formulated. The third sphere may include this intellectual domain as well, but it also encompasses a deeper emotional dimension which cannot be seized upon by intellectual analysis alone. The didactic, *moralizing* tendency of a large number of the epigrams points toward this "hidden" sphere. The following are examples of these epigrams:

"Der beste Narr"

Narren giebt's überall auf der Welt,
Doch Jedem sein eigner am besten gefällt.
(II/7, p. 324)

"Adelsinstinkt"

Wappen ließ die edle Dame in des Säuglings
　Windeln nähen,
Und das Kind starb an Verstopfung, eh' es noch
　sein Schild gesehen.
Lernt daraus, wie viel es heiße, adelig geboren
　sein!
Nur aus noblem Bauchinstinkte hielt das Kind den
　Adel rein.
(II/55, p. 331)

"Bauer und Edelmann"

Wenn der Bauer wird ein Edelmann,
So guckt er den Pflug mit Brillen an.
(II/58, p. 332)

"Gebet ohne Arbeit"

Faul in der Arbeit, fleißig im Beten,
Orgelspiel ohne Balgentreten.
(III/76, p. 361)

"Memento Mori!"
Springst du freudig durch die Thüre in dein
  neugebautes Haus,
Denk', aus dieser selben Thüre tragen sie dich
  einst heraus.

(I/60, p. 316)

Whether it is the nobility, religious hypocrites, or fools who are made to look absurd, the method is the same. Through a clearly drawn characterization one or another extreme is portrayed, and through this comic portrayal it is criticized. The moral, however, that is the higher sphere in which such extremes are recognized as such and overcome, lives *not* in the facts described in the epigram itself, but rather in the reaction of our feelings when confronted by them. The author's intent may thus be properly described as didactic. The higher realm lies hidden behind the lines, and herein consists the peculiarly acid cut of the epigrams: through a conceptually formulated example we are suddenly and unceremoniously ejected from the habits of our everyday thinking and are forced to recognize the deeper dimension which lies hidden behind them. Only upon awakening to this dimension do we become conscious of the more basically human implications of the situation portrayed. This higher sphere of reconciliation, which is only implied in the epigrams (in which it nevertheless functions with impressive directness), animates the better lyrical poems as well. In these it is often itself portrayed, as in the metaphor of the ocean in "Selbstbeschauung."

The Middle Position

In order to overcome the tension inherent in the polarities of experience, Wilhelm Müller consistently seeks, consciously or subconsciously, a middle position. The latter consists not in the intellectual scheme which encompasses the extremes, but in a sphere of experience qualitatively distinct from them. In this third sphere, thoughts and feelings are united on a higher level. This may be experienced in the epigrams, in individual poems, and also in the central themes and metaphors which run through the song-cycles we have discussed. A clear example is the psychological threat which besets the soul, now as the temptation to give up the struggle of existence and dissolve into formlessness ("Müllerin"), now as the tendency to abandon contact with the world and die the spiritual death of isolation in a soul-landscape of frozen form ("Winterreise"). The reconciliation of these extremes, which is presented in the "Frühlingskranz," flows from a position which, as we have seen, unites the two poles and transforms them into a higher harmony, a *living form*. This middle position is characterized by a conscious "opening" of the heart as an organ of perception which releases new possibilities of experience, both inward and outward. The same phenomenon we found to be at work in the poem "Die liebe Farbe." In that poem the color green, which earlier was bearer of the polar opposite associations "gut/böse," was seen from a new metaphorical middle position. Through its enlarged scope of experience, the latter liberates the quality "green" from the static polarity of associations and enables the reader to sense its heightening in a sphere behind death.[1]

It is not accidental that the whole question of the middle position which overcomes and reconciles opposites should come into focus through the world of *color*. A qualitative experience of color swings between the opposing sensations of warm and cold, major and minor, sympathy and antipathy. The color green, which of course comes about through the uniting of the warmth of yellow and the coldness of blue, represents a natural center from which both extremes are held in balance. Inwardly grasped, this whole phenomenon presents the most natural metaphor for the extent and fluidity of the emotional "coloration" of the soul's experience. This insight provides the poet with an inexhaustible wealth of metaphorical possibilities. It also lies at the very core of Wilhelm Müller's poetic imagination. It is the true "window" through which we are able to observe the activity which is peculiarly characteristic of this poet's relationship to the creative process. He has, moreover, himself formulated this stance in one of the epigrams:

"Das Prisma"

Dem Prisma gleicht des Dichters Seele, in welcher Freud' und Leid sich bricht
Mit hellen und mit trüben Strahlen zu buntem Regenbogenlicht.

(I/98, p. 322)

The psychological polarity of the experiences of sympathy and antipathy, expressed repeatedly in the formula "Freud' und Leid," is here clearly identified with the world of colors. The poet's soul is a finely ground lens which enables him to experience the colors not quantitatively, by wave-length, but qualitatively, as "deeds and sufferings of light" in the Goethean sense.

An even deeper secret of Wilhelm Müller's poetic imagination lies concealed in this beautiful image of the prism. We have observed that a strong sense of proportion, what we might term an "architectural" sense, is everywhere in evidence in Müller's clear eye for form. At the same time, he is known and loved for the musical sensitivity which runs through all his poems. Interestingly enough, these two fundamental creative tendencies are brought together in the most extraordinarily clear focus in this epigram. The prism itself may be appropriately described as a highly refined architectural form which, in its selfless transparency, allows the light to stream through it, and to bring to manifestation the musical scale of the play of colors.

In speaking in the foregoing paragraph of the "play of colors," we have pointed in another way to the "middle position" under discussion. In purely philosophical terms, Friedrich Schiller describes the qualitative or aesthetic mode of experience which mediates between the extremes of form and matter, the "*Spiel*trieb." Only in this middle realm of his being does man escape the tyranny of one-sidedness and feel himself as a free being.[2]

In its highest manifestation, an awakening in this middle region is for Wilhelm Müller a moment of self-knowledge. The great celebration in nature, which in "Das Frühlingsmahl" reveals the complete interpenetration of spirit and matter, stands before the human being as an example of the new harmony which he must strive to establish within his own being. The sacramental act described in that poem is consciously recognized by man in outer nature and in his own soul and is thereby completed. With the death of the purely earthly existence, a seed of higher life begins to develop ("That und Wille"). The poem "Selbstbeschauung," in which death is portrayed through a juxtaposition of images which are reconciled in the embracing metaphor of the watery heavens, is therefore very appropriately named. An awakening in the "middle sphere," which harmonizes extremes and liberates man's creative spirit, is an awakening to one's self as a complete human being. The greatest heightening of this "awakening" is seen by Müller in death.

The Heart as Lens of the Soul

The soul's "prism," of which Müller speaks, is usually present in only a rudimentary form, clouded by the "tobenden Stürmen der Brust" ("Selbstbeschauung"). Its purification is gradually accomplished by the education of the heart, of which the "Frühlingskranz" speaks ("Die Fenster auf, die Herzen auf!"). As the heart is developed into what one might term a "lens of the soul," the light may find entrance through it. This process is not brought about intellectually. It involves rather the ability to achieve the childlike quality of soul which we noted in the "Frühlingskranz" and which finds expression in the poem "Weihnachten" (Hatfield, pp. 389-390):

> Leget ab die weisen Falten
> Die um eure Stirnen walten,
> Wird das Kind euch gerne sehn.

Naturally, it is tempting to dismiss the importance attached by Müller to the heart and to the quality of childhood as trivial sentimentality. Trivial and sentimental elements are of course found in profusion in his works. But it is important to develop a sense of discrimination in evaluating the material, for to dismiss *en masse* all poems which touch on the qualities we have been discussing would amount to a misreading of the works. Such poems as "Weihnachten" spring from a quality of heart and mind which is, in the best sense of the word, "childlike" in its inwardness. In his biography, Gustav Schwab writes of a report concerning the poet, delivered by the latter's friend, Simolin:

> "Dieser [Simolin] kehrte zu Weinachten 1825 nach Dessau zurück, und hatte jetzt, wie seine Mittheilungen sagen, 'die beste Gelegenheit, Müllers einfache, kindliche Natur kennen zu lernen. An dem großen Christfeste einer Kinderwelt spielte auch er im Geben und Empfangen so selig mit, daß man das Reinmenschliche, Unschuldige seines reichen Gemüthes hier am besten zu erkennen im Stande war.'"[3]

The Poet in the Service of the Spirit

The childlike quality of listening with the heart is itself at work throughout Wilhelm Müller's poetry. It explains for instance his love for the simple peasantry which comes to expression in his Italian poems[4] and travel notes[5] or the "Muscheln von der Insel Rügen."[6] A particularly arresting psychological depth is reached, as we have seen, in "Die Winterreise," in which the poet converses with his heart (cf. "Die Post"). Yet the poems of this cycle lead logically into an inner void, for the wanderer here merely addresses the heart from without, rather than undertaking its transformation from within. The "prism" is not yet sufficiently transparent (i.e., "selfless") to receive a higher inspiration. When it *is* transformed, however, the light of the Christian festivals streams into the soul from within ("Weihnachten") and from without ("Pfingsten"). On this level the task of the poet is deepened. He no longer collects mussels, combining them into wreaths, but gathers the blossoms which God has bestowed upon man as holy "letters" ("Der Peripatetiker"). He places his energies in the service of the spirit. One of Müller's earliest poems, "Mein erstes Sonett" (1814) is a poem about a poem.[7] The sonnet is described allegorically as a flower with fourteen petals—a blossom "composed" by man. In the "Frühlingskranz" the blossoms are "composed" by God and are to be gathered and "read" (*gelesen*) by man, the poet. The *Urbild* of the poet, the primordial bard, is thus God; and it devolves upon man to carry on His work.

In view of the foregoing it will perhaps not be surprising to discover that Müller particularly admired Calderon. This poet, he felt, overcame the workings of "blind destiny" (i.e., the mood of the "Winterreise") through his service in the name of the "eternal Gardener." The sonnet "Calderon," which appeared in 1823 (although it may have been written earlier), brings clearly to expression Müller's admiration for the poet as servant of the spirit:

Calderon

Was in der Menschenseele dunklen Tiefen
Mit Lust und Schmerz, mit Haß und Liebe waltet,
Bis es der Knospe feste Hüllen spaltet,
In der die Keime aller Thaten schliefen;

Und die Gewalten, die an's Licht sie riefen,
Die Hand, die Blüthen abbricht und entfaltet,
Und aus den Blüthen Früchte dann gestaltet:
Das sind des Erdendrama's Hiroglyphen.

Du hast sie uns mit Blumenschrift geschrieben
In einem weiten, hellen Zaubergarten,
Aus dem wir in des Himmels Fernen schauen.

Kein blindes Schicksal ist zurück geblieben;

Des ew'gen Gärtners Hände selber warten
Der Blumen in den bunten Lebensauen.
(Hatfield, p. 397)

Calderon is here seen as a poet who forms the "blossoms" of the "eternal Gardener" into a "Blumenschrift," a flower-language which reveals the "hieroglyphs of earthly drama" — i.e., the mysterious workings of destiny. These forces are on the one hand those of the inner, emotional sphere (again seen as polarities: "Lust und Schmerz," ... "Haß und Liebe") and on the other hand the powerful forces ("Gewalten") of destiny, set into motion by the former. Human destiny is here viewed in the image of a plant which unfolds under the watchful care of the "eternal Gardener." The poet who fulfills his calling in this deeper sense is viewed by Müller as a servant of the Gardener Whose desire it is that the world shall be transformed and spiritually perfected.

The Wellspring of Intuition

The poet who transforms his heart into a prism through which the light of spirit may shine harmonizes the opposite tendencies of formlessness and of frozen form and creates, on a higher level, a new living form. This he is enabled to achieve through his newly deepened intuitive experience of the spirit inherent in himself and in the world about him. This new posture is therefore a conscious experience in an intuitive element of *"sculptural fluidity."* If this expression sounds paradoxical, it is the proper one, for it contains both elements and yet allows neither to gain the ascendency. Nothing in Wilhelm Müller's poetic imagination can be forced into the mold of a rigid system. Everything develops organically between such polarities as spirit/matter, inward/outward, light/darkness, etc. In this sense there is an attunement unconsciously at work in this poet which is akin to the highly conscious posture cultivated by Goethe in his relationship to the world (cf. the *Metamorphose der Pflanzen* or the *Farbenlehre*). This is *not* to be construed as what obviously would be an absurd comparison between the two poets, nor do we seek to enhance Müller's stature by backhanded association. It is simply an objective fact that a similarity exists in the manner described above. The crucial difference is of course that the posture in question is present in Müller in only the most rudimentary form and largely in the realm of feeling, whereas in Goethe it is raised into the light of thinking and developed into a clearly articulated method.

The spiritual element of "sculptural fluidity," as a medium created and experienced by the conscious "I" of man, points to an intimate mystery. This medium, flowing at the innermost core of the poet's soul, may be described as the true wellspring of intuition. The picture of this wellspring, formed by the activity of man himself (a spring which simultaneously encloses and reveals the intuitions which live in the process of poetic creation), is most clearly captured in the sonnet "Juli" (Hatfield, p. 57). It is included in a collection of poems entitled "Die Monate" (1818). In these poems, which with the exception of "Juli" are of little interest, the quality of each month is described, usually through personification. In July the sun has reached its zenith and there is experienced what one might term an "hour of Pan" in the year. It is an hour in which, under the burning sun, the human being is in danger of slipping into a dreamy state of mind. Such a mood plays into the present poem, yet the picture is drawn in full wakefulness. The sonnet form itself testifies to a high degree of control. Within the confines of this very conscious form there gradually arises a most extraordinary image which, in the final stanza, gives birth to a magically dreamlike vision:

Juli

Auf kühlen Bergen, an des Meeres Strande,
Ist dir ein heitrer Gartensitz bereitet,
Nicht allzu eng', auch nicht zu weit verbreitet:
Man liebt sich einzuschränken auf dem Lande.

Ein junger Quell im Bett von weichem Sande
Ist zierlich durch die Gänge hingeleitet,

> Bis er betrogen in ein Becken gleitet,
> Das ihm versteckt der Blumenhain am Rande.
>
> Da muß er, eingezwängt in schlanker Säule,
> Aufsteigen aus dem runden Marmorrunde,
> Und auf der Höhe sich in Schaum zerstäuben.
>
> Das Moosbett winkt zu mittäglicher Weile:
> Es schlummert Alles, nur im klaren Grunde
> Seh' ich die goldnen Fischlein Spiele treiben.

Müller has here drawn a picture whose implications are deeper than he can consciously have realized. The locale itself is significant. Between the polar opposite landscapes of the ocean and the solid mountains lies a *garden*. We have pointed to Müller's use of the ocean (in "Muscheln von der Insel Rügen") as a metaphor for the sea of imagination out of which the poet draws his songs.[8] Just at the point at which the polarities of landscape, the formless (ocean) and the solidly formed (mountains) come together, this "Gartensitz," a section of landscape transformed through man's aesthetic activity, is established. The place is described as cheerful ("heiter") and (polarity again) "Nicht allzu eng', auch nicht zu weit verbreitet." Then comes the very important word "einzuschränken" (line four). In the self-imposed limitations of the aesthetically transformed landscape man creates a friendly sphere which is less overwhelming than either the mountains or the ocean alone. It is clearly a sphere of *art* which, created by man, surrounds him with a truly "human" environment.

The theme of the artistic transformation of the elements of nature in this garden is now elaborated. The gardener has won control over a "young spring" (i.e., a part of the watery element whose *Urbild* is the nearby ocean) and controls this personified water at will. The water is led through the walkways until it must flow into a basin. Here it feels itself deceived, for the basin is hidden by flowers. We are now no longer surprised to find the image of the flowers appearing in this context. Man the artist is here himself a gardener.

We must now put aside all "realistic" reflections on the scene at hand and meditate on the imagery as such, for, experienced as metaphor, it gives expression to the innermost secrets of the processes of creation within man's consciousness. In the third stanza the picture of the fountain is precisely drawn. It is a living, flowing "source," formed by man. The fact that it feels deceived is irrelevant, for the water is now controlled by the conscious human being, whose will it must obey. The fountain is a work of art of a unique type. Through the conscious activity of the "I" of man, the formless element is forced into a particular form, but this is a living form, in constant motion. We spoke above of a deeper awareness in consciousness, one which may be likened to a living experience in an element of "sculptural fluidity." Here it is. Out of this inner posture the artist draws his inspiration and creates his works of art.

After having interpreted the poem in this manner the author was pleased to find his thoughts indirectly corroborated in an article by Wilhelm Schneider on Conrad Ferdinand Meyer's "Der römische Brunnen."[9] Schneider speaks of the image of the fountain as "die Vorstellung einer strömenden Ruhe, ... auf jedes echte Kunstwerk anwendbar." (p. 118). He goes on to discuss in detail the possible objection that such a symbolic interpretation might amount to *over*interpretation. He very properly points out that the question as to whether or not the poet was consciously aware of the deeper symbolic content which he placed into such a poem is irrelevant. Poets often give expression to imagery of whose deeper significance they are only partially aware, the important point being that one come to the realization: "... *es hat in ihnen gedacht* ..." (pp. 119-120). As Schneider very correctly states, "Hier rühren wir an ein Geheimnis des dichterischen Schaffens und der Poesie überhaupt." (p. 120).

In the last stanza the mood shifts as we penetrate into the depths of the experience. The gaze falls onto the bed of moss. As the sun attains its zenith, the midday hour is reached—the hour which with respect to the day is the same as is the month of July for the year. All is asleep, yet the poet is awake. In this magical moment the fountain continues to stream, and the poet lowers his gaze down into the depths, the "klaren Grund." It is the depths *not* of the ocean, but of the *basin*, which holds the water of the fountain. In other words, the point is here reached at which the conscious artist (encompassing, through the "lyrical I," the poet, the gardener, the creative artist in general) is enabled to gaze down *behind* his own activity. The living "source" which he has in his control continues to stream, and in this midday moment of unusually tranquil consciousness the artist may look down into the depths of his wellspring. And what does he see? "... im klaren Grunde / Seh ich die goldnen Fischlein Spiele treiben." Nearly every word is of importance here. The poet has called forth a picture of the inner wellspring of intuition at the heart of his poetic imagination, where all "sculptural fluidity," all "living form" is produced by the "I." The little golden fishes which appear and dart about at just this moment are an enchanting vision indeed. In this moment in which all nature is asleep they appear almost as a precious distillation of the imaginative world of dream itself. We will not venture to identify them more specifically, for this would only lead to an unwarranted narrowing of the experience. They are silent creatures of the watery element, alive and golden – somehow living images of a radiant and precious realm caught sight of by the poet in this moment of heightened perceptivity.

It is of particular interest that just in this last line of the poem the word "ich" appears, the "I" whose activity has found expression in the imagery of the poem itself. As we have noted, it is the "lyrisches Ich" which encompasses that of the poet, the landscape gardener and the reader himself. It is the "I" of any human being who is spiritually creative. We note also the verb *sehen*, which is attached to this "I" ("Seh' ich ...") and recall to mind the last two lines of "Erlösung" (the poem which also contains the image of the fish): "Und das Aug' ist aufgeweckt, / Welches durch den Äther sieht." The poet has transformed the inner "prism," the eye of the soul. This inner eye becomes transparent and allows him to build up the whole sonnet to a final line which focuses upon the magical beauty of the little golden fish.

What is it that these little fish are doing? They are "playing" ("treiben Spiele"). By quite a different route, we have already had occasion to direct our attention to the significance of *play* ("das Spielen"). In the Schillerian sense it is the activity in which man experiences the freedom of his humanity. Every act of artistic creation flows ultimately ("im Grunde") from such a "playful" attitude of mind. Thus the basic inner necessity of the imagery in this poem dictates that the little golden fish do exactly what they *must* do: play. Once this is properly understood, the living picture which this sonnet quite innocently presents of the secrets of the creative process in the poet's consciousness is complete. The fountain, formed by the active human "I," creates a sphere in which a very earnest "Spiel" is revealed to the wakeful eye, for in the mysterious image of the "goldnen Fischlein" we are granted a first inkling of the intuitive world which lies behind the creative process. In the face of such a naïvely conceived poem as this, which lays before us in clear metaphorical terms the mystery of the creative "I" (and does so with an uncanny consistency of detail), one can justifiably feel a certain reverential wonderment.

We have noted that for Wilhelm Müller the sunlight of Whitsuntide, which strews the divine "letters" over the earth, is in the Christian sense a revelation of truth ("Der Peripatetiker," "Sonntag"). A strong sense of individuality is evident in Müller's biography and also in his works.[10] In the final analysis, he felt allegiance to but one authority—his own sovereign "I." Within this "I" there speaks the voice of conscience, which he sought to perceive. As an ideal toward which to strive, he saw before him the picture of the "I" which transforms the heart into an organ of perception, a prism of the soul through which the light of spirit may break. And in the light there lived for Müller the truth ("Wahrheit"), the Light of the World. Out of the deepest wellsprings of his being, Müller felt himself united with the message of Christianity. Shortly before his death, he wrote a letter to his good friend Simolin. Gustav Schwab has passed on to us a lengthy passage from this letter, which contains a very personal confession, not intended for publication. The following is an extract from this passage:

> *Wahrheit* ist ein Grundzug meiner Natur, meines Charakters und meines Lebens. Ohne *Wahrheit* gibt es für mich keine Tugend, keine Schönheit, keine Liebe und keine Freundschaft. Ich kann daher, auch auf die Gefahr einen Freund zu verlieren, nicht unwahr sein.

After a few more personal remarks he continues:

> ... denn Freunde können wohl über einzelne Meinungen, Ansichten, Maximen verschieden fühlen, denken und urtheilen; aber, wenn es das *Höchste* gilt—die Principien über Gut und Schlecht, Edel und Unedel, Recht und Unrecht: da kan keine Differenz zwischen ihnen obwalten. Daher ist auch hier durchaus von keiner Übereilung, Heftigkeit und dergleichen die Rede. Die Grundsätze, die ich gegen Dich ausgesprochen, sind *allgemein*, die in mir so fest stehen, wie der Glaube an Gott, Tugend und Gerechtigkeit.[11]

From the center of his being Müller speaks the words which in the poem "Sonntag" (Hatfield, pp. 388-389) are spoken by the angels: "Geist der Wahrheit uns umwehe ..."

A large portion of Wilhelm Müller's lyrical production must remain for us today of only limited interest. Much of what he wrote was frivolous and appears in a dated, conventional garb. We hope to have demonstrated, however, that his better works are of considerable artistic merit. In conceiving them Müller drew upon rich inner resources. The more sensitive and perceptive side of his nature was anything but superficial. He tells us himself, in one of his epigrams (I/95, Hatfield, p.

321), that in his more serious hours he sought to draw his poetic inspiration from a deep source:

"Tiefe und Klarheit"

Wie hell und klar auch sei der Himmel, du kannst
   doch seinen Grund nicht sehn.
Je tiefer das Gedicht ich schöpfe, je lichter
   wird es vor dir stehn.

Appendix

Die schöne Müllerin

Der Dichter, als Prolog

Ich lad' euch, schöne Damen, kluge Herrn,
Und die ihr hört und schaut was Gutes gern,
Zu einem funkelnagelneuen Spiel
Im allerfunkelnagelneusten Styl;
Schlicht ausgedrechselt, kunstlos zugestutzt,
Mit edler deutscher Rohheit aufgeputzt,
Keck wie ein Bursch im Stadtsoldatenstrauß,
Dazu wohl auch ein wenig fromm für's Haus:
Das mag genug mir zur Empfehlung sein,
Wem die behagt, der trete nur herein.
Erhoffe, weil es grad' ist Winterzeit,
Thut euch ein Stündlein hier im Grün nicht Leid;
Denn wißt es nur, daß heut' in meinem Lied
Der Lenz mit allen seinen Blumen blüht.
Im Freien geht die freie Handlung vor,
In reiner Luft, weit von der Städte Thor,
Durch Wald und Feld, in Gründen, auf den Höhn;
Und was nur in vier Wänden darf geschehn,
Das schaut ihr halb durch's offne Fenster an,
So ist der Kunst und euch genug gethan.

Doch wenn ihr nach des Spiels Personen fragt,
So kann ich euch, den Musen sei's geklagt,
Nur *eine* präsentiren recht und ächt,
Das ist ein junger blonder Müllersknecht.
Denn, ob der Bach zuletzt ein Wort auch spricht,
So wird ein Bach deshalb Person noch nicht.
Drum nehmt nur heut' das Monodram vorlieb:
Wer mehr giebt, als er hat, der heißt ein Dieb.

Auch ist dafür die Szene reich geziert,
Mit grünem Sammet unten tapeziert,

Der ist mit tausend Blumen bunt gestickt,
Und Weg und Steg darüber ausgedrückt.
Die Sonne strahlt von oben hell herein
Und bricht in Thau und Thränen ihren Schein,
Und auch der Mond blickt aus der Wolken Flor
Schwermüthig, wie's die Mode will, hervor.
Den Hintergrund umkränzt ein hoher Wald,
Der Hund schlägt an, das muntre Jagdhorn schallt;
Hier stürzt vom schroffen Fels der junge Quell
Und fließt im Thal als Bächlein silberhell;
Das Mühlrad braust, die Werke klappern drein,
Man hört die Vöglein kaum im nahen Hain.
Drum denkt, wenn euch zu rauh manch Liedchen klingt,
Daß das Lokal es also mit sich bringt.
Doch, was das Schönste bei den Rädern ist,
Das wird euch sagen mein Monodramist;
Verrieth' ich's euch, verdürb' ich ihm das Spiel:
Gehabt euch wohl und amüsirt euch viel!

Wanderschaft

Das Wandern ist des Müllers Lust,
   Das Wandern!
Das muß ein schlechter Müller sein,
Dem niemals fiel das Wandern ein,
   Das Wandern.

Vom Wasser haben wir's gelernt,
   Vom Wasser!
Das hat nicht Rast bei Tag und Nacht,
Ist stets auf Wanderschaft bedacht,
   Das Wasser.

Das sehn wir auch den Rädern ab,
   Den Rädern!
Die gar nicht gerne stille stehn,
Die sich mein Tag nicht müde drehn,
   Die Räder.

Die Steine selbst, so schwer sie sind,
   Die Steine!
Sie tanzen mit den muntern Reihn
Und wollen gar noch schneller sein,
   Die Steine.

O Wandern, Wandern, meine Lust,
O Wandern!
Herr Meister und Frau Meisterin,
Laßt mich in Frieden weiter ziehn
Und wandern.

Wohin?

Ich hört' ein Bächlein rauschen
Wohl aus dem Felsenquell,
Hinab zum Thale rauschen
So frisch und wunderhell.

Ich weiß nicht, wie mir wurde,
Nicht, wer den Rath mir gab,
Ich mußte gleich hinunter
Mit meinem Wanderstab.

Hinunter und immer weiter,
Und immer dem Bache nach,
Und immer frischer rauschte,
Und immer heller der Bach.

Ist das denn meine Straße?
O Bächlein, sprich, wohin?
Du hast mit deinem Rauschen
Mir ganz berauscht den Sinn.

Was sag' ich denn von Rauschen?
Das kann kein Rauschen sein:
Es singen wohl die Nixen
Dort unten ihren Reihn.

Laß singen, Gesell, laß rauschen,
Und wandre fröhlich nach!
Es gehn ja Mühlenräder
In jedem klaren Bach.

Halt!

Eine Mühle seh' ich blicken
Aus den Erlen heraus,
Durch Rauschen und Singen
Bricht Rädergebraus.

Ei willkommen, ei willkommen,
Süßer Mühlengesang!
Und das Haus, wie so traulich!
Und die Fenster, wie blank!

Und die Sonne, wie helle
Vom Himmel sie scheint!
Ei, Bächlein, liebes Bächlein,
War es also gemeint?

Danksagung an den Bach

War es also gemeint,
Mein rauschender Freund,
Dein Singen, dein Klingen,
War es also gemeint?

Zur Müllerin hin!
So lautet der Sinn.
Gelt, hab' ich's verstanden?
Zur Müllerin hin!

Hat *sie* dich geschickt?
Oder hast mich berückt?
Das möcht' ich noch wissen,
Ob *sie* dich geschickt.

Nun wie's auch mag sein,
Ich gebe mich drein:
Was ich such', ist gefunden,
Wie's immer mag sein.

Nach Arbeit ich frug,
Nun hab' ich genug,
Für die Hände, für's Herze
Vollauf genug!

Am Feierabend

Hätt' ich tausend
Arme zu rühren!
Könnt' ich brausend
Die Räder führen!

Könnt' ich wehen
Durch alle Haine!
Könnt' ich drehen
Alle Steine!
Daß die schöne Müllerin
Merkte meinen treuen Sinn!

Ach, wie ist mein Arm so schwach!
Was ich hebe, was ich trage,
Was ich schneide, was ich schlage,
Jeder Knappe thut es nach.
Und da sitz' ich in der großen Runde,
Zu der stillen kühlen Feierstunde,
Und der Meister spricht zu Allen:
Euer Werk hat mir gefallen;
Und das liebe Mädchen sagt
Allen eine gute Nacht.

Der Neugierige

Ich frage keine Blume,
Ich frage keinen Stern,
Sie können mir nicht sagen,
Was ich erführ' so gern.

Ich bin ja auch kein Gärtner,
Die Sterne stehn zu hoch;
Mein Bächlein will ich fragen,
Ob mich mein Herz belog.

O Bächlein meiner Liebe,
Wie bist du heut' so stumm!
Will ja nur Eines wissen,
Ein Wörtchen um und um.

Ja, heißt das eine Wörtchen,
Das andre heißet Nein,
Die beiden Wörtchen schließen
Die ganze Welt mir ein.

O Bächlein meiner Liebe,
Was bist du wunderlich!
Will's ja nicht weiter sagen,
Sag', Bächlein, liebt sie mich?

Das Mühlenleben

Seh' ich sie am Bache sitzen,
Wenn sie Fliegennetze strickt,
Oder Sonntags für die Fenster
Frische Wiesenblumen pflückt;

Seh' ich sie zum Garten wandeln,
Mit dem Körbchen in der Hand,
Nach den ersten Beeren spähen
An der grünen Dornenwand:

Dann wird's eng' in meiner Mühle,
Alle Mauern ziehn sich ein,
Und ich möchte flugs ein Fischer,
Jäger oder Gärtner sein.

Und der Steine lustig Pfeifen,
Und des Wasserrads Gebraus,
Und der Werke emsig Klappern,
'S jagt mich fast zum Thor hinaus.

Aber wenn in guter Stunde
Plaudernd sie zum Burschen tritt,
Und als kluges Kind des Hauses
Seitwärts nach dem Rechten sieht;

Und verständig lobt den Einen,
Daß der Andre merken mag,
Wie er's besser treiben solle,
Geht er ihrem Danke nach —

Keiner fühlt sich recht getroffen,
Und doch schießt sie nimmer fehl,
Jeder muß von Schonung sagen,
Und doch hat sie keinen Hehl.

Keiner wünscht, sie möchte gehen,
Steht sie auch als Herrin da,
Und fast wie das Auge Gottes
Ist ihr Bild uns immer nah. —

Ei, da mag das Mühlenleben
Wohl des Liedes würdig sein,
Und die Räder, Stein' und Stampfen
Stimmen als Begleitung ein.

Alles geht in schönem Tanze
Auf und ab, und ein und aus:
Gott gesegne mir das Handwerk
Und des guten Meisters Haus!

Ungeduld

Ich schnitt' es gern in alle Rinden ein,
Ich grüb' es gern in jeden Kieselstein,
Ich möcht' es sä'n auf jedes frische Beet
Mit Kressensamen, der es schnell verräth,
Auf jeden weißen Zettel möcht' ich's schreiben:
Dein ist mein Herz, und soll es ewig bleiben.

Ich möcht' mir ziehen einen jungen Staar,
Bis daß er spräch' die Worte rein und klar,
Bis er sie spräch' mit meines Mundes Klang,
Mit meines Herzens vollem, heißem Drang;
Dann säng' er hell durch ihre Fensterscheiben:
Dein ist mein Herz, und soll es ewig bleiben.

Den Morgenwinden möcht' ich's hauchen ein,
Ich möcht' es säuseln durch den regen Hain;
O, leuchtet' es aus jedem Blumenstern!
Trüg' es der Duft zu ihr von nah und fern!
Ihr Wogen, könnt ihr nichts als Räder treiben?
Dein ist mein Herz, und soll es ewig bleiben.

Ich meint', es müßt' in meinen Augen stehn,
Auf meinen Wangen müßt' man's brennen sehn,
Zu lesen wär's auf meinem stummen Mund,
Ein jeder Athemzug gäb's laut ihr kund;
Und sie merkt nichts von all' dem bangen Treiben:
Dein ist mein Herz, und soll es ewig bleiben!

Morgengruß

Guten Morgen, schöne Müllerin!
Wo steckst du gleich das Köpfchen hin,
Als wär' dir was geschehen?
Verdrießt dich denn mein Gruß so schwer?
Verstört dich denn mein Blick so sehr?
So muß ich wieder gehen.

O laß mich nur von ferne stehn,
Nach deinem lieben Fenster sehn,
Von ferne, ganz von ferne!
Du blondes Köpfchen, komm hervor!
Hervor aus eurem runden Thor,
Ihr blauen Morgensterne!

Ihr schlummertrunknen Äugelein,
Ihr thaubetrübten Blümelein,
Was scheuet ihr die Sonne?
Hat es die Nacht so gut gemeint,
Daß ihr euch schließt und bückt und weint
Nach ihrer stillen Wonne?

Nun schüttelt ab der Träume Flor,
Und hebt euch frisch und frei empor
In Gottes hellen Morgen!
Die Lerche wirbelt in der Luft,
Und aus dem tiefen Herzen ruft
Die Liebe Leid und Sorgen.

Des Müllers Blumen

Am Bach viel kleine Blumen stehn,
Aus hellen blauen Augen sehn;
Der Bach der ist des Müllers Freund,
Und hellblau Liebchens Auge scheint,
Drum sind es meine Blumen.

Dicht unter ihrem Fensterlein
Da pflanz' ich meine Blumen ein,
Da ruft ihr zu, wenn Alles schweigt,
Wenn sich ihr Haupt zum Schlummer neigt,
Ihr wißt ja, was ich meine.

Und wenn sie thät die Äuglein zu,
Und schläft in süßer, süßer Ruh',
Dann lispelt als ein Traumgesicht
Ihr zu: Vergiß, vergiß mein nicht!
Das ist es, was ich meine.

Und schließt sie früh die Laden auf,
Dann schaut mit Liebesblick hinauf:
Der Thau in euren Äugelein,
Das sollen meine Thränen sein,
Die will auf euch weinen.

Thränenregen

Wir saßen so traulich beisammen
Im kühlen Erlendach,
Wir schauten so traulich zusammen
Hinab in den rieselnden Bach.

Der Mond war auch gekommen,
Die Sternlein hinterdrein,
Und schauten so traulich zusammen
In den silbernen Spiegel hinein.

Ich sah nach keinem Monde,
Nach keinem Sternenschein,
Ich schaute nach ihrem Bilde,
Nach ihren Augen allein.

Und sahe sie nicken und blicken
Herauf aus dem seligen Bach,
Die Blümlein am Ufer, die blauen,
Sie nickten und blickten ihr nach.

Und in den Bach versunken
Der ganze Himmel schien,
Und wollte mich mit hinunter
In siene Tiefe ziehn.

Und über den Wolken und Sternen
Da rieselte munter der Bach,
Und rief mit Singen und Klingen:
Geselle, Geselle, mir nach!

Da gingen die Augen mir über,
Da ward es im Spiegel so kraus;
Sie sprach: Es kommt ein Regen,
Ade, ich geh' nach Haus.

Mein!

Bächlein, laß dein Rauschen sein!
Räder, stellt eur Brausen ein!
All' ihr muntern Waldvögelein,
Groß und klein,
Endet eure Melodein!

Durch den Hain
Aus und ein
Schalle heut' *ein* Reim allein:
Die geliebte Müllerin ist *mein*!
Mein!
Frühling, sind das alle deine Blümelein?
Sonne, hast du keinen hellern Schein?
Ach, so muß ich ganz allein,
Mit dem seligen Worte *mein*,
Unverstanden in der weiten Schöpfung sein!

                Pause

Meine Laute hab' ich gehängt an die Wand,
Hab' sie umschlungen mit einem grünen Band —
Ich kann nicht mehr singen, mein Herz ist zu voll,
Weiß nicht, wie ich's in Reime zwingen soll.
Meiner Sehnsucht allerheißesten Schmerz
Durft' ich aushauchen in Liederscherz,
Und wie ich klagte so süß und fein,
Meint' ich doch, mein Leiden wär' nicht klein.
Ei, wie groß ist wohl meines Glückes Last,
Daß kein Klang auf Erden es in sich faßt?

Nun, liebe Laute, ruh' an dem Nagel hier!
Und weht ein Lüftchen über die Saiten dir,
Und streift eine Biene mit ihren Flügeln dich,
Da wird mir bange und es durchschauert mich.
Warum ließ ich das Band auch hängen so lang'?
Oft fliegt's um die Saiten mit seufzendem Klang.
Ist es der Nachklang meiner Liebespein?
Soll es das Vorspiel neuer Lieder sein?

           Mit dem grünen Lautenbande

"Schad' um das schöne grüne Band,
Daß es verbleicht hier an der Wand,
Ich hab' das Grün so gern!"
So sprachst du, Liebchen, heut' zu mir;
Gleich knüpf' ich's ab und send' es dir:
Nun hab' das Grüne gern!

Ist auch dein ganzer Liebster weiß,
Soll Grün doch haben seinen Preis,
Und ich auch hab' es gern.
Weil unsre Lieb' ist immergrün,
Weil grün der Hoffnung Fernen blühn,
Drum haben wir es gern.

Nun schlingst du in die Locken dein
Das grüne Band gefällig ein,
Du hast ja 's Grün so gern.
Dann weiß ich, wo die Hoffnung wohnt,
Dann weiß ich, wo die Liebe thront,
Dann hab' ich's Grün erst gern.

Der Jäger

Was sucht denn der Jäger am Mühlbach hier?
Bleib', trotziger Jäger, in deinem Revier!
Hier giebt es kein Wild zu jagen für dich,
Hier wohnt nur ein Rehlein, ein zahmes, für mich.
Und willst du das zärtliche Rehlein sehn,
So laß deine Büchsen im Walde stehn,
Und laß deine klaffenden Hunde zu Haus,
Und laß auf dem Horne den Saus und Braus,
Und scheere vom Kinne das struppige Haar,
Sonst scheut sich im Garten das Rehlein fürwahr.

Doch besser, du bliebest im Walde dazu,
Und ließest die Mühlen und Müller in Ruh'.
Was taugen die Fischlein im grünen Gezweig?
Was will denn das Eichhorn im bläulichen Teich?
Drum bleibe, du trotziger Jäger, im Hain,
Und laß mich mit meinen drei Rädern allein;
Und willst meinem Schätzchen dich machen beliebt,
So wisse, mein Freund, was ihr Herzchen betrübt:
Die Eber, die kommen zu Nacht aus dem Hain,
Und brechen in ihren Kohlgarten ein,
Und treten und wühlen herum in dem Feld:
Die Eber die schieße, du Jägerheld!

Eifersucht und Stolz

Wohin so schnell, so kraus, so wild, mein lieber Bach?
Eilst du voll Zorn dem frechen Bruder Jäger nach?

Kehr' um, kehr' um, und schilt erst deine Müllerin
Für ihren leichten, losen, kleinen Flattersinn.
Sahst du sie gestern Abend nicht am Thore stehn,
Mit langem Halse nach der großen Straße sehn?
Wenn von dem Fang der Jäger lustig zieht nach Haus,
Da steckt kein sittsam Kind den Kopf zum Fenster 'naus.
Geh', Bächlein, hin und sag' ihr das, doch sag' ihr nicht,
Hörst du, kein Wort, von meinem traurigen Gesicht;
Sag' ihr: Er schnitzt bei mir sich eine Pfeif' aus Rohr,
Und bläst den Kindern schöne Tänz' und Lieder vor.

Erster Schmerz, letzter Scherz

Nun sitz' am Bache nieder
Mit deinem hellen Rohr,
Und blas' den lieben Kindern
Die schönen Lieder vor.

Die Lust ist ja verrauschet,
Das Leid hat immer Zeit:
Nun singe neue Lieder
Von alter Seligkeit.

Noch blühn die alten Blumen,
Noch rauscht der alte Bach,
Es scheint die liebe Sonne
Noch wie am ersten Tag.

Die Fensterscheiben glänzen
Im klaren Morgenschein,
Und hinter den Fensterscheiben
Da sitzt die Liebste mein.

Ein Jäger, ein grüner Jäger,
Der liegt in ihrem Arm —
Ei, Bach, wie lustig du rauschest!
Ei, Sonne, wie scheinst du so warm!

Ich will einen Strauß dir pflücken,
Herzliebste, von buntem Klee,
Den sollst du mir stellen an's Fenster,
Damit ich den Jäger nicht seh'.

Ich will mit Rosenblättern
Den Mühlensteg bestreun:
Der Steg hat mich getragen
Zu dir, Herzliebste mein!

Und wenn der stolze Jäger
Ein Blättchen mir zertritt,
Dann stürz', o Steg, zusammen
Und nimm den Grünen mit!

Und trag' ihn auf dem Rücken
In's Meer, mit gutem Wind,
Nach einer fernen Insel,
Wo keine Mädchen sind.

Herzliebste, das Vergessen,
Es kommt dir ja nicht schwer —
Willst du den Müller wieder?
Vergißt dich nimmermehr.

Die liebe Farbe

In Grün will ich mich kleiden,
In grüne Thränenweiden,
Mein Schatz hat 's Grün so gern.
Will suchen einen Zypressenhain,
Eine Heide voll grünem Rosmarein,
Mein Schatz hat 's Grün so gern.

Wohlauf zum fröhlichen Jagen!
Wohlauf durch Heid' und Hagen!
Mein Schatz hat 's Jagen so gern.
Das Wild, das ich jage, das ist der Tod,
Die Heide, die heiß' ich die Liebesnoth,
Mein Schatz hat 's Jagen so gern.

Grabt mir ein Grab im Wasen,
Deckt mich mit grünem Rasen,
Mein Schatz hat 's Grün so gern.
Kein Kreuzlein schwarz, kein Blümlein bunt,
Grün, Alles grün so rings und rund!
Mein Schatz hat 's Grün so gern.

Die böse Farbe

Ich möchte ziehn in die Welt hinaus,
Hinaus in die weite Welt,
Wenn's nur so grün, so grün nicht wär'
Da draußen in Wald und Feld!

Ich möchte die grünen Blätter all'
Pflücken von jedem Zweig,
Ich möchte die grünen Gräser all'
Weinen ganz todtenbleich.

Ach Grün, du böse Farbe du,
Was siehst mich immer an,
So stolz, so keck, so schadenfroh,
Mich armen weißen Mann?

Ich möchte liegen vor ihrer Thür,
In Sturm und Regen und Schnee,
Und singen ganz leise bei Tag und Nacht
Das eine Wörtchen Ade!

Horch, wenn im Wald ein Jagdhorn ruft,
Da klingt ihr Fensterlein,
Und schaut sie auch nach mir nicht aus,
Darf ich doch schauen hinein.

O binde von der Stirn dir ab
Das grüne, grüne Band,
Ade, Ade! und reiche mir
Zum Abschied deine Hand!

Blümlein Vergißmein

Was treibt mich jeden Morgen
So tief in's Holz hinein?
Was frommt mir, mich zu bergen
Im unbelauschten Hain?

Es blüht auf allen Fluren
Blümlein *Vergiß mein nicht*,
Es schaut vom heitern Himmel
Herab in blauem Licht.

Und soll ich's niedertreten,
Bebt mir der Fuß zurück,
Es fleht aus jedem Kelche
Ein wohlbekannter Blick.

Weißt du, in welchem Garten
Blümlein *Vergiß mein* steht?
Das Blümlein muß ich suchen,
Wie auch die Straße geht.

'S ist nicht für Mädchenbusen,
So schön sieht es nicht aus:
Schwarz, schwarz ist seine Farbe
Es paßt in keinen Strauß.

Hat keine grüne Blätter,
Hat keinen Blüthenduft,
Es windet sich am Boden
In nächtig dumpfer Luft.

Wächst auch an einem Ufer,
Doch unten fließt kein Bach,
Und willst das Blümlein pflücken,
Dich zieht der Abgrund nach.

Das ist der rechte Garten,
Ein schwarzer, schwarzer Flor:
Darauf magst du dich betten —
Schleuß zu das Gartenthor!

  Trockne Blumen

 Ihr Blümlein alle,
 Die sie mir gab,
 Euch soll man legen
 Mit mir in's Grab.

 Wie seht ihr alle
 Mich an so weh,
 Als ob ihr wüßtet,
 Wie mir gescheh'?

 Ihr Blümlein alle,
 Wie welk, wie blaß?
 Ihr Blümlein alle,
 Wovon so naß?

 Ach, Thränen machen
 Nicht maiengrün,
 Machen todte Liebe
 Nicht wieder blühn.

 Und Lenz wird kommen,
 Und Winter wird gehn,
 Und Blümlein werden
 Im Grase stehn,

Und Blümlein liegen
In meinem Grab,
Die Blümlein alle,
Die sie mir gab.

Und wenn sie wandelt
Am Hügel vorbei,
Und denkt im Herzen:
Der meint' es treu!

Dann Blümlein alle,
Heraus, heraus!
Der Mai ist kommen,
Der Winter ist aus.

Der Müller und der Bach

    Der Müller

Wo ein treues Herze
In Liebe vergeht,
Da welken die Lilien
Auf jedem Beet.

Da muß in die Wolken
Der Vollmond gehn,
Damit seine Thränen
Die Menschen nicht sehn.

Da halten die Englein
Die Augen sich zu,
Und schluchzen und singen
Die Seele zu Ruh'.

    Der Bach

Und wenn sich die Liebe
Dem Schmerz entringt,
Ein Sternlein, ein neues,
Am Himmel erblinkt.

Da springen drei Rosen,
Halb roth, halb weiß,
Die welken nicht wieder,
Aus Dornenreis.

Und die Engelein schneiden
Die Flügel sich ab,
Und gehn alle Morgen
Zur Erde hinab.

Der Müller

Ach, Bächlein, liebes Bächlein,
Du meinst es so gut:
Ach, Bächlein, aber weißt du,
Wie Liebe thut?

Ach, unten, da unten,
Die kühle Ruh'!
Ach, Bächlein, liebes Bächlein,
So singe nur zu.

Des Baches Wiegenlied

Gute Ruh', gute Ruh'!
Thu' die Augen zu!
Wandrer, du müder, du bist zu Haus.
Die Treu' ist hier,
Sollst liegen bei mir,
Bis das Meer will trinken die Bächlein aus.

Will betten dich kühl,
Auf weichem Pfühl,
In dem blauen krystallenen Kämmerlein.
Heran, heran,
Was wiegen kann,
Woget und wieget den Knaben mir ein!

Wenn ein Jagdhorn schallt
Aus dem grünen Wald,
Will ich sausen und brausen wohl um dich her.
Blickt nicht herein,
Blaue Blümelein!
Ihr macht meinem Schläfer die Träume so schwer.

Hinweg, hinweg
Von dem Mühlensteg,
Böses Mägdlein, daß ihn dein Schatten nicht weckt!
Wirf mir herein
Dein Tüchlein fein,
Daß ich die Augen ihm halte bedeckt!

Gute Nacht, gute Nacht!
Bis Alles wacht,
Schlaf' aus deine Freude, schlaf' aus dein Leid!
Der Vollmond steigt,
Der Nebel weicht,
Und der Himmel da oben, wie ist er so weit!

Der Dichter, als Epilog

Weil gern man schließt mit einer runden Zahl,
Tret' ich noch einmal in den vollen Saal,
Als letztes, fünf und zwanzigstes Gedicht,
Als Epilog, der gern das Klügste spricht.
Doch pfuschte mir der Bach in's Handwerk schon
Mit seiner Leichenred' im nassen Ton.
Aus solchem hohlen Wasserorgelschall
Zieht Jeder selbst sich besser die Moral;
Ich geb' es auf, und lasse diesen Zwist,
Weil Widerspruch nicht meines Amtes ist.

So hab' ich denn nichts lieber hier zu thun,
Als euch zum Schluß zu wünschen, wohl zu ruhn.
Wir blasen unsre Sonn' und Sternlein aus —
Nun findet euch im Dunkel gut nach Haus,
Und wollt ihr träumen einen leichten Traum,
So denkt an Mühlenrad und Wasserschaum,
Wenn ihr die Augen schließt zu langer Nacht,
Bis es den Kopf zum Drehen euch gebracht.
Und wer ein Mädchen führt an seiner Hand,
Der bitte scheidend um ein Liebespfand,
Und giebt sie heute, was sie oft versagt,
So sei des treuen Müllers treu gedacht
Bei jedem Händedruck, bei jedem Kuß
Bei jedem heißen Herzensüberfluß:
Geb' ihm die Liebe für sein kurzes Leid
In eurem Busen lange Seligkeit!

Die Winterreise

Gute Nacht

Fremd bin ich eingezogen,
Fremd zieh' ich wieder aus.
Der Mai war mir gewogen
Mit manchem Blumenstrauß.
Das Mädchen sprach von Liebe,
Die Mutter gar von Eh' —
Nun ist die Welt so trübe,
Der Weg gehüllt in Schnee.

Ich kann zu meiner Reisen
Nicht wählen mit der Zeit:
Muß selbst den Weg mir weisen
In dieser Dunkelheit.
Es zieht ein Mondenschatten
Als mein Gefährte mit,
Und auf den weißen Matten
Such' ich des Wildes Tritt.

Was soll ich länger weilen,
Bis man mich trieb' hinaus?
Laß irre Hunde heulen
Vor ihres Herren Haus!
Die Liebe liebt das Wandern, —
Gott hat sie so gemacht —
Von Einem zu dem Andern —
Fein Liebchen, Gute Nacht!

Will dich im Traum nicht stören,
Wär' Schad' um deine Ruh',
Sollst meinen Tritt nicht hören —
Sacht, sacht die Thüre zu!

Ich schreibe nur im Gehen
An's Thor noch gute Nacht,
Damit du mögest sehen,
Ich hab' an dich gedacht.

Die Wetterfahne

Der Wind spielt mit der Wetterfahne
Auf meines schönen Liebchens Haus.
Da dacht' ich schon in meinem Wahne,
Sie pfiff' den armen Flüchtling aus.

Er hätt' es ehr bemerken sollen,
Des Hauses aufgestecktes Schild,
So hätt' er nimmer suchen wollen
Im Haus ein treues Frauenbild.

Der Wind spielt drinnen mit den Herzen,
Wie auf dem Dach, nur nicht so laut.
Was fragen sie nach meinen Schmerzen?
Ihr Kind ist eine reiche Braut.

Gefrorene Thränen

Gefrorne Tropfen fallen
Von meinen Wangen ab:
Und ist's mir denn entgangen,
Daß ich geweinet hab'?

Ei Thränen, meine Thränen,
Und seid ihr gar so lau,
Daß ihr erstarrt zu Eise,
Wie kühler Morgenthau?

Und dringt doch aus der Quelle
Der Brust so glühend heiß,
Als wolltet ihr zerschmelzen
Des ganzen Winters Eis.

Erstarrung

Ich such' im Schnee vergebens
Nach ihrer Tritte Spur,
Hier, wo wir oft gewandelt
Selbander durch die Flur.

Ich will den Boden küssen,
Durchdringen Eis und Schnee
Mit meinen heißen Thränen,
Bis ich die Erde seh'.

Wo find' ich eine Blüthe,
Wo find' ich grünes Gras?
Die Blumen sind erstorben,
Der Rasen sieht so blaß.

Soll denn kein Angedenken
Ich nehmen mit von hier?
Wenn meine Schmerzen schweigen,
Wer sagt mir dann von ihr?

Mein Herz ist wie erfroren,
Kalt starrt ihr Bild darin:
Schmilzt je das Herz mir wieder,
Fließt auch das Bild dahin.

Der Lindenbaum

Am Brunnen vor dem Thore
Da steht ein Lindenbaum:
Ich träumt' in seinem Schatten
So manchen süßen Traum.

Ich schnitt in seine Rinde
So manches liebe Wort;
Es zog in Freud' und Leide
Zu ihm mich immer fort.

Ich mußt' auch heute wandern
Vorbei in tiefer Nacht,
Da hab' ich noch im Dunkel
Die Augen zugemacht.

Und seine Zweige rauschten,
Als riefen sie mir zu:

Komm her zu mir, Geselle,
Hier findst du deine Ruh'!

Die kalten Winde bliesen
Mir grad' in's Angesicht,
Der Hut flog mir vom Kopfe,
Ich wendete mich nicht.

Nun bin ich manche Stunde
Entfernt von jenem Ort,
Und immer hör' ich's rauschen:
Du fändest Ruhe dort!

Die Post

Von der Straße her ein Posthorn klingt.
Was hat es, daß es so hoch aufspringt,
   Mein Herz?

Die Post bringt keinen Brief für dich:
Was drängst du denn so wunderlich,
   Mein Herz?

Nun ja, die Post kömmt aus der Stadt,
Wo ich ein liebes Liebchen hatt',
   Mein Herz!

Willst wohl einmal hinübersehn,
Und fragen, wie es dort mag gehn,
   Mein Herz?

Wasserfluth

Manche Thrän' aus meinen Augen
Ist gefallen in den Schnee;
Seine kalten Flocken saugen
Durstig ein das heiße Weh.

Wann die Gräser sprossen wollen,
Weht daher ein lauer Wind,
Und das Eis zerspringt in Schollen,
Und der weiche Schnee zerrinnt.

Schnee, du weißt von meinem Sehnen:
Sag' mir, wohin geht dein Lauf?
Folge nach nur meinen Thränen,
Nimmt dich bald das Bächlein auf.

Wirst mit ihm die Stadt durchziehen,
Muntre Straßen ein und aus:
Fühlst du meine Thränen glühen,
Da ist meiner Liebsten Haus.

Auf dem Flusse

Der du so lustig rauschtest,
Du heller, wilder Fluß,
Wie still bist du geworden,
Giebst keinen Scheidegruß.

Mit harter, starrer Rinde
Hast du dich überdeckt,
Liegst kalt und unbeweglich
Im Sande hingestreckt.

In deine Decke grab' ich
Mit einem spitzen Stein
Den Namen meiner Liebsten
Und Stund' und Tag hinein:

Den Tag des ersten Grußes,
Den Tag, an dem ich ging,
Um Nam' und Zahlen windet
Sich ein zerbrochner Ring.

Mein Herz, in diesem Bache
Erkennst du nun dein Bild?
Ob's unter seiner Rinde
Wohl auch so reißend schwillt?

Rückblick

Es brennt mir unter beiden Sohlen,
Tret' ich auch schon auf Eis und Schnee.
Ich möcht' nicht wieder Athem holen,
Bis ich nicht mehr die Thürme seh'.

Hab' mich an jedem Stein gestoßen,
So eilt' ich zu der Stadt hinaus;
Die Krähen warfen Bäll' und Schloßen
Auf meinen Hut von jedem Haus.

Wie anders hast du mich empfangen,
Du Stadt der Unbeständigkeit!
An deinen blanken Fenstern sangen
Die Lerch' und Nachtigall im Streit.

Die runden Lindenbäume blühten,
Die klaren Rinnen rauschten hell,
Und ach, zwei Mädchenaugen glühten! —
Da war's geschehn um dich, Gesell!

Kömmt mir der Tag in die Gedanken,
Möcht' ich noch einmal rückwärts sehn,
Möcht' ich zurücke wieder wanken,
Vor *ihrem* Hause stille stehn.

Der greise Kopf

Der Reif hatt' einen weißen Schein
Mir über's Haar gestreuet.
Da meint' ich schon ein Greis zu sein,
Und hab' mich sehr gefreuet.

Doch bald ist er hinweggethaut,
Hab' wieder schwarze Haare,
Daß mir's vor meiner Jugend graut —
Wie weit noch bis zur Bahre!

Vom Abendroth zum Morgenlicht
Ward mancher Kopf zum Greise.
Wer glaubt's? Und meiner ward es nicht
Auf dieser ganzen Reise!

Die Krähe

Eine Krähe war mit mir
Aus der Stadt gezogen,
Ist bis heute für und für
Um mein Haupt geflogen.

Krähe, wunderliches Thier,
Willst mich nicht verlassen?
Meinst wohl bald als Beute hier
Meinen Leib zu fassen?

Nun, es wird nicht weit mehr gehn
An dem Wanderstabe.
Krähe, laß mich endlich sehn
Treue bis zum Grabe!

Letzte Hoffnung

Hier und da ist an den Bäumen
Noch ein buntes Blatt zu sehn,
Und ich bleibe vor den Bäumen
Oftmals in Gedanken stehn.

Schaue nach dem einen Blatte,
Hänge meine Hoffnung dran;
Spielt der Wind mit meinem Blatte,
Zittr' ich, was ich zittern kann.

Ach, und fällt das Blatt zu Boden,
Fällt mit ihm die Hoffnung ab,
Fall' ich selber mit zu Boden,
Wein' auf meiner Hoffnung Grab.

Im Dorfe

Es bellen die Hunde, es rasseln die Ketten.
Die Menschen schnarchen in ihren Betten,
Träumen sich Manches, was sie nicht haben,
Thun sich im Guten und Argen erlaben:
Und morgen früh ist Alles zerflossen. —
Je nun, sie haben ihr Theil genossen,
Und hoffen, was sie noch übrig ließen,
Doch wieder zu finden auf ihren Kissen.

Bellt mich nur fort, ihr wachen Hunde,
Laßt mich nicht ruhn in der Schlummerstunde!
Ich bin zu Ende mit allen Träumen —
Was will ich unter den Schläfern säumen?

Der stürmische Morgen

Wie hat der Sturm zerrissen
Des Himmels graues Kleid!
Die Wolkenfetzen flattern
Umher in mattem Streit.

Und rothe Feuerflammen
Ziehn zwischen ihnen hin.
Das nenn' ich einen Morgen
So recht nach meinem Sinn!

Mein Herz sieht an dem Himmel
Gemalt sein eignes Bild —
Es ist nichts als der Winter,
Der Winter kalt und wild!

Täuschung

Ein Licht tanzt freundlich vor mir her;
Ich folg' ihm nach die Kreuz und Quer;
Ich folg' ihm gern, und seh's ihm an,
Daß es verlockt den Wandersmann.
Ach, wer wie ich so elend ist,
Giebt gern sich hin der bunten List,
Die hinter Eis und Nacht und Graus
Ihm weist ein helles, warmes Haus,
Und eine liebe Seele drin —
Nur Täuschung ist für mich Gewinn!

Der Wegweiser

Was vermeid' ich denn die Wege,
Wo die andren Wandrer gehn,
Suche mir versteckte Stege
Durch verschneite Felsenhöhn?

Habe ja doch nichts begangen,
Daß ich Menschen sollte scheun —
Welch ein thörichtes Verlangen
Treibt mich in die Wüstenein?

Weiser stehen auf den Straßen,
Weisen auf die Städte zu,
Und ich wandre sonder Maßen,
Ohne Ruh', und suche Ruh'.

Einen Weiser seh' ich stehen
Unverrückt vor meinem Blick;
Eine Straße muß ich gehen,
Die noch Keiner ging zurück.

Das Wirthshaus

Auf einen Todtenacker
Hat mich mein Weg gebracht.
Allhier will ich einkehren:
Hab' ich bei mir gedacht.

Ihr grünen Todtenkränze
Könnt wohl die Zeichen sein,
Die müde Wandrer laden
In's kühle Wirthshaus ein.

Sind denn in diesem Hause
Die Kammern all' besetzt?
Bin matt zum Niedersinken
Und tödtlich schwer verletzt.

O unbarmherz'ge Schenke,
Doch weisest du mich ab?
Nun weiter denn, nur weiter,
Mein treuer Wanderstab!

Das Irrlicht

In die tiefsten Felsengründe
Lockte mich ein Irrlicht hin:
Wie ich einen Ausgang finde,
Liegt nicht schwer mir in dem Sinn.

Bin gewohnt das irre Gehen,
'S führt ja jeder Weg zum Ziel:
Unsre Freuden, unsre Wehen,
Alles eines Irrlichts Spiel!

Durch des Bergstroms trockne Rinnen
Wind' ich ruhig mich hinab—
Jeder Strom wird 's Meer gewinnen,
Jedes Leiden auch ein Grab.

Rast

Nun merk' ich erst, wie müd' ich bin,
Da ich zur Ruh' mich lege;
Das Wandern hielt mich munter hin
Auf unwirthbarem Wege.

Die Füße frugen nicht nach Rast,
Es war zu kalt zum Stehen,
Der Rücken fühlte keine Last,
Der Sturm half fort mich wehen.

In eines Köhlers engem Haus
Hab' Obdach ich gefunden;
Doch meine Glieder ruhn nicht aus:
So brennen ihre Wunden.

Auch du, mein Herz, im Kampf und Sturm
So wild und so verwegen,
Fühlst in der Still' erst deinen Wurm
Mit heißem Stich sich regen!

Die Nebensonnen

Drei Sonnen sah ich am Himmel stehn,
Hab' lang' und fest sie angesehn;
Und sie auch standen da so stier,
Als könnten sie nicht weg von mir.
Ach, *meine* Sonnen seid ihr nicht!
Schaut Andren doch in's Angesicht!
Ja, neulich hatt' ich auch wohl drei:
Nun sind hinab die besten zwei.
Ging' nur die dritt' erst hinterdrein!
Im Dunkel wird mir wohler sein.

Frühlingstraum

Ich träumte von bunten Blumen,
So wie sie wohl blühen im Mai,

Ich träumte von grünen Wiesen,
Von lustigem Vogelgeschrei.

Und als die Hähne krähten,
Da ward mein Auge wach;
Da war es kalt und finster,
Es schrieen die Raben vom Dach.

Doch an den Fensterscheiben
Wer malte die Blätter da?
Ihr lacht wohl über den Träumer,
Der Blumen im Winter sah?

Ich träumte von Lieb' um Liebe,
Von einer schönen Maid,
Von Herzen und von Küssen,
Von Wonn' und Seligkeit.

Und als die Hähne krähten,
Da ward mein Herze wach;
Nun sitz' ich hier alleine
Und denke dem Traume nach.

Die Augen schließ' ich wieder,
Noch schlägt das Herz so warm.
Wann grünt ihr Blätter am Fenster?
Wann halt' ich dich, Liebchen, im Arm?

Einsamkeit

Wie eine trübe Wolke
Durch heitre Lüfte geht,
Wann in der Tanne Wipfel
Ein mattes Lüftchen weht:

So zieh' ich meine Straße
Dahin mit trägem Fuß,
Durch helles, frohes Leben,
Einsam und ohne Gruß.

Ach, daß die Luft so ruhig!
Ach, daß die Welt so licht!
Als noch die Stürme tobten,
War ich so elend nicht.

Muth!

Fliegt der Schnee mir in's Gesicht,
Schüttl' ich ihn herunter.
Wenn mein Herz im Busen spricht,
Sing' ich hell und munter.

Höre nicht, was es mir sagt,
Habe keine Ohren.
Fühle nicht, was es mir klagt,
Klagen ist für Thoren.

Lustig in die Welt hinein
Gegen Wind und Wetter!
Will kein Gott auf Erden sein,
Sind wir selber Götter.

Der Leiermann

Drüben hinter'm Dorfe
Steht ein Leiermann,
Und mit starren Fingern
Dreht er was er kann.

Barfuß auf dem Eise
Schwankt er hin und her;
Und sein kleiner Teller
Bleibt ihm immer leer.

Keiner mag ihn hören,
Keiner sieht ihn an;
Und die Hunde brummen
Um den alten Mann.

Und er läßt es gehen
Alles, wie es will,
Dreht, und seine Leier
Steht ihm nimmer still.

Wunderlicher Alter,
Soll ich mit dir gehn?
Willst zu meinen Liedern
Deine Leier drehn?

Frühlingskranz aus dem Plauenschen Grunde bei Dresden

Frühlingseinzug

Die Fenster auf, die Herzen auf!
  Geschwinde! Geschwinde!
Der alte Winter will heraus,
Er trippelt ängstlich durch das Haus,
Er windet bang' sich in der Brust,
Und kramt zusammen seinen Wust
  Geschwinde, geschwinde.

Die Fenster auf, die Herzen auf!
  Geschwinde! Geschwinde!
Er spürt den Frühling vor dem Thor,
Der will ihn zupfen bei dem Ohr,
Ihn zausen an dem weißen Bart
Nach solcher wilden Buben Art,
  Geschwinde, geschwinde.

Die Fenster auf, die Herzen auf!
  Geschwinde! Geschwinde!
Der Frühling pocht und klopft ja schon —
Horcht, horcht, es ist sein lieber Ton!
Er pocht und klopfet, was er kann,
Mit kleinen Blumenknospen an,
  Geschwinde, geschwinde.

Die Fenster auf, die Herzen auf!
  Geschwinde! Geschwinde!
Und wenn ihr noch nicht öffnen wollt,
Er hat viel Dienerschaft im Sold,
Die ruft er sich zur Hülfe her,
Und pocht und klopfet immer mehr,
  Geschwinde, geschwinde.

Die Fenster auf, die Herzen auf!
Geschwinde! Geschwinde!
Es kömmt der Junker Morgenwind,
Ein bausebackig rotes Kind,
Und bläst, das Alles klingt und klirrt,
Bis seinem Herrn geöffnet wird,
 Geschwinde, geschwinde.

Die Fenster auf, die Herzen auf!
 Geschwinde! Geschwinde!
Es kömmt der Ritter Sonnenschein,
Der bricht mit goldnen Lanzen ein,
Der sanfte Schmeichler Blüthenhauch
Schleicht durch die engsten Ritzen auch,
 Geschwinde, geschwinde.

Die Fenster auf, die Herzen auf!
Geschwinde! Geschwinde!
Zum Angriff schlägt die Nachtigall,
Und horch, und horch, ein Wiederhall,
Ein Wiederhall aus meiner Brust!
Herein, herein, du Frühlingslust,
 Geschwinde, geschwinde!

Kinderfrühling

Wollt euch nicht so schnell belauben,
Wälder, und mir wieder rauben
Diesen lieben Sonnenschein,
Den so lang' ich mußte missen,
Bis die Schleier er zerrissen,
Die den Himmel hüllten ein.

Zwischen knospenvollen Zweigen
Seh' ich auf und nieder steigen
Kleiner Vöglein buntes Heer,
Seh' sie schnäbeln, seh' sie picken,
Und die schwanken Reiser nicken,
Denen ihre Last zu schwer.

Und der klare blaue Himmel
Breitet hinter dem Gewimmel
Sich in stillem Frieden aus.
Wie durch kleine Fenstergitter
Spielt die Sonne mit Gezitter
Durch der Zweige Flechtenhaus.

Halbbegrünet stehn die Hecken,
Und die Nachbarskinder necken
Durch die dürren Lücken sich,
Bis das Mädchen röther glühet
Und zu dichtern Stellen fliehet
Vor dem Knaben jüngferlich.

Frühling, heute noch ein Knabe,
Treibet auf des Winters Grabe
Mit den Kindern seinen Scherz,
Bis der Gott der süßen Triebe
Mit dem Flammenpfeil der Liebe
Ihm durchbohrt das kleine Herz.

Kinderlust

Nun feget aus den alten Staub
Und macht die Laube blank!
Laßt ja kein schwarzes Winterlaub
Mir liegen auf der Bank!

Die erste weiße Blüthe flog
Mir heut' in's Angesicht.
Willkommen, Lenz! Ich lebe noch
Und weiß von Leide nicht.

Und schaue hell, wie du, hinein
In Gottes schöne Welt,
Und möcnt' ein kleiner Bube sein
Und kollern durch das Feld.

O seht, da plätschern schon am See
Die lieben Kindelein,
Und ziehn die Hemdchen in die Höh',
Und wollen gern hinein.

Wie lockt der warme Sonnenschein,
Der auf dem Spiegel ruht!
Da ist kein Fuß zu weich, zu klein,
Er probt, wie 's Wasser thut.

Ich sitz' und seh' dem Spiele zu,
Und spiel' im Herzen auch.
Du lieber Lenz, ein Kind bist du,
Und übest Kinderbrauch.

Wie viel du hast, du weißt es kaum,
Und schüttest Alles aus.
Nehmt, Kinder, nehmt! Es ist kein Traum!
Es kommt aus Gottes Haus.

Und wenn du nun ganz fertig bist,
Hast keine Blume mehr,
Dann gehst du wieder ohne Frist,
Kein Abschied wird dir schwer.

Und rufst dem Bruder Sommer zu:
Bringst du die Früchte her?
Was ich versprach, das halte du!
Ei, ei, dein Korb ist schwer!

Die Brautnacht

Es hat geflammt die ganze Nacht
Am hohen Himmelsbogen,
Wie eines Feuerspieles Pracht
Hat es die Luft durchflogen.

Und nieder sank es tief und schwer
Mit ahnungsvoller Schwüle,
Ein dumpfes Rollen zog daher
Und sprach von ferner Kühle.

Da fielen Tropfen warm und mild,
Wie lang' erstickte Thränen;
Die Erde trank, doch ungestillt
Blieb noch ihr heißes Sehnen.

Und sieh, der Morgen steigt empor —
Welch Wunder ist geschehen?
In ihrem vollen Blüthenflor
Seh' ich die Erde stehen.

O Wunder, wer hat das vollbracht?
Der Knospen spröde Hülle
Wer brach sie auf in *einer* Nacht
Zu solcher Liebesfülle?

O still, o still, und merket doch
Der Blüthen scheues Bangen!
Ein rother Schauer zittert noch
Um ihre frischen Wangen.

O still, und fragt den Bräutigam,
Den Lenz, den kühnen Freier,
Der diese Nacht zur Erde kam,
Nach ihrer Hochzeitfeier.

Das Frühlingsmahl

Wer hat die weißen Tücher
Gebreitet über das Land?
Die weißen duftenden Tücher
Mit ihrem grünen Rand?

Und hat darüber gezogen
Das hohe blaue Zelt?
Darunter den bunten Teppich
Gelagert über das Feld?

Er ist es selbst gewesen,
Der gute reiche Wirth
Des Himmels und der Erden,
Der nimmer ärmer wird.

Er hat gedeckt die Tische
In seinem weiten Saal,
Und ruft was lebet und webet,
Zum großen Frühlingsmahl.

Wie strömt's aus allen Blüthen
Herab von Strauch und Baum!
Und jede Blüth' ein Becher
Voll süßer Düfte Schaum.

Hört ihr des Wirthes Stimme?
Heran, was kriecht und fliegt,
Was geht und steht auf Erden,
Was unter den Wogen sich wiegt!

Und du, mein Himmelspilger,
Hier trinke trunken dich,
Und sinke selig nieder
Auf's Knie und denk' an mich!

Erlösung

Wie dem Fische wird zu Muth,
Wenn des Flusses Rinde springt,
Und des jungen Lebens Gluth
Durch des Eises Decke dringt.

Also wie aus Kerkerqual
Fühlet meine Brust sich frei,
Wenn des Frühlings Sonnenstrahl
Reißt der Wolken Zelt entzwei.

Und das Dach ist abgedeckt,
Das mich von dem Himmel schied,
Und das Aug' ist aufgeweckt,
Welches durch den Äther sieht.

Morgenlied

Wer schlägt so rasch an die Fenster mir
Mit schwanken grünen Zweigen?
Der junge Morgenwind ist hier
Und will sich lustig zeigen.

Heraus, heraus, du Menschensohn,
So ruft der kecke Geselle,
Es schwärmt von Frühlingswonnen schon
Vor deiner Kammerschwelle.

Hörst du die Käfer summen nicht?
Hörst du das Glas nicht klirren,
Wenn sie, betäubt von Duft und Licht,
Hart an die Scheiben schwirren?

Die Sonnenstrahlen stehlen sich
Behende durch Blätter und Ranken,
Und necken auf deinem Lager dich
Mit blendendem Schweben und Schwanken.

Die Nachtigall ist heiser fast,
So lang' hat sie gesungen,
Und weil du sie gehört nicht hast,
Ist sie vom Baum gesprungen.

Da schlug ich mit dem leeren Zweig
An deine Fensterscheiben.
Heraus, heraus in des Frühlings Reich!
Er wird nicht lange mehr bleiben.

Der Peripatetiker

Alles will ich nun verlernen,
Was mich lehrte das Papier.
Schwarze, steife, stumme Lettern,
Sagt, was wollt ihr noch von mir?

In die grüne Wanderschule
Ruft mich ein Philosophus,
Einer, der sich nennt mit Rechten
Ein Peripatetikus.

Denn er zieht mit seiner Lehre
Durch die Länder ein und aus,
Schlägt in Wald und Feld und Garten
Auf sein wunderbares Haus.

Eine große Schaar von Schülern
Folgt ihm durch die weite Welt,
Vöglein in den blauen Lüften,
Vöglein in dem grünen Zelt.

Und sie zwitschern unverdrossen
Ihres Meisters Weisheit nach;
Was sie gestern erst erfahren,
Lehren sie an diesem Tag.

Und der Weise aller Weisen
Kollert sich im weichen Gras,
Wiegt sich auf den schwanken Zweigen,
Als ob Alles wär' ein Spaß.

Also streut er seine Lettern,
Weiß und roth und gelb und blau,
Ohne Wahl, mit vollen Händen,
Über Berg und Thal und Au'.

Lest, o lest die lieben Schriften
Voller Wahrheit, voller Lust,
Brüder, lest und stürzt euch selig
An des Lehrers warme Brust!

Die Forelle

In der hellen Felsenwelle
Schwimmt die muntere Forelle,
Und in wildem Übermuth
Guckt sie aus der kühlen Fluth,
Sucht, gelockt von lichten Scheinen,
Nach den weißen Kieselsteinen,
Die das seichte Bächlein kaum
Überspritzt mit Staub und Schaum.

Sieh doch, sieh, wie kann sie hüpfen
Und so unverlegen schlüpfen
Durch den höchsten Klippensteg,
Grad', als wäre das ihr Weg!
Und schon will sie nicht mehr eilen,
Will ein wenig sich verweilen,
Zu erproben, wie es thut,
Sich zu sonnen aus der Fluth.

Über einem blanken Steine
Wälzt sie sich im Sonnenscheine,
Und die Strahlen kitzeln sie
In der Haut, sie weiß nicht wie,
Weiß in wähligem Behagen
Nicht, ob sie es soll ertragen,
Oder vor der fremden Gluth
Retten sich in ihre Fluth.

Kleine muntere Forelle
Weile noch an dieser Stelle
Und sei meine Lehrerin:
Lehre mir den leichten Sinn,
Über Klippen weg zu hüpfen,
Durch des Lebens Drang zu schlüpfen,
Und zu gehn, ob's kühlt, ob's brennt,
Frisch in jedes Element.

Das Brautkleid

Die Flur hat angezogen
Ein grünes seidenes Kleid,
Die leichten schillernden Falten
Umfliegen sie weit und breit.

Und unter der flatternden Hülle
Schlägt ihre warme Brust,
Die Winde wollen sie kühlen
Und verglühen sich selber in Lust.

Es zucken die Sonnenstrahlen
Herunter mit blitzendem Brand,
Als möchten sie gern ihr versengen
Das neidische grüne Gewand.

Sie ruft: Ihr Strahlen, ihr Winde,
Mein Kleid laßt unversehrt!
Es ward von meinem Liebsten
Zum Brautschmuck mir bescheert.

Der Mai, so heißt mein Liebster,
Er gab es zu tragen mir,
Er sprach: Du sollst es tragen,
So lang' ich bleibe bei dir.

Und wenn ich von dir scheide,
So werd' es gelb vor Gram,
Dann laß es von den Menschen
Dir ausziehn ohne Scham.

Und leg' als nackte Witwe
Dich nieder mit deinem Leid,
Bis daß ich wieder kehre
Und bring' ein neues Kleid.

Die Biene

Biene, dich könnt' ich beneiden,
Könnte Neid im Frühling wachsen,
Wenn ich dich versunken sehe,
Immer leiser leiser summend,
In dem rosenrothen Kelche
Einer jungen Apfelblüthe.
Als die Knospe wollte springen
Und verschämt es noch nicht wagte,
In die helle Welt zu schauen,
Jetzo kamst du hergeflogen
Und ersahest dir die Knospe;
Und noch eh' ein Strahl der Sonne
Und ein Flatterhauch des Zephyrs

Ihren Kelch berühren konnte,
Hingest du daran und sogest.
Sauge, sauge! — Schwer und müde
Fliegst du heim nach deiner Zelle:
Hast dein Tagewerk vollendet,
Hast gesorgt auch für den Winter!

Pfingsten

O heilige Frühlingswonne,
Du sinkest nieder,
Strahlend und flimmernd
In himmlischen Schauern,
Auf alle Berge,
In alle Thäler,
In jede Menschenbrust!
Ja, du bist es,
Geist Gottes,
Du gießest dich aus
Über die Welt!
Soll ich auf die sonnige Höhe steigen
Und beten?
Soll ich in dem dunkeln Thale liegen
Und sinnen?
O tritt sanft, mein Fuß,
Daß du den Wurm nicht trestest,
Der unter dir
Sich freuet des sonnigen Lebens!
Und du, hoch schlagende Brust,
Halt' an den Athem,
Daß du die Mücke
Nicht in dich ziehest,
Die sich wieget im Strahle
Vor deinem Munde!

Xenion

An Friedrich Grafen von Kalckreuth

Meine Muse liebt das Reisen,
Kehret gern bei Freunden ein:
Neue Wirthe, neue Weisen,
Und die neuesten sind dein.

In dem grünen Felsenthale
Hinter dem Forellenbach
Saß sie jüngst an deinem Mahle,
Unter deinem treuen Dach.

Und der Frühling streute nieder
Seine Gaben in das Gras.
Meine Muse suchte Lieder,
Wenn sie Maienblumen las.

Sieh, der Kranz, den sie gewunden
Von den liebsten, die sie fand,
Dankbar ist er angebunden
An des Wirthes Giebelwand.

Notes

Introduction

[1] Cf. Philip S. Allen, "Wilhelm Müller and Italian Popular Poetry," *Modern Language Notes*, XIV, No. 6 (1899), 165-166.

[2] Cf. Philip S. Allen, "Wilhelm Müller and the German Volkslied" (Diss. University of Chicago, 1899). Reprinted in *Journal of English and Germanic Philology*, II (1898-99), 283-322; III (1901), No. 1, 35-91; III, No. 4, 431-491.

[3] A recent article by K. G. Just points to the possibility of a reëvaluation of Müller's poetry: Klaus Günther Just, "Wilhelm Müllers Liederzyklen 'Die schöne Müllerin' und 'Die Winterreise,'" *Zeitschrift für deutsche Philologie*, LXXXIII (1964), 452-471. Reprinted in Just, *Übergänge. Probleme und Gestalten der Literatur* (Bern and München: Francke, 1966), pp. 133-152.

[4] F. Max Müller, *Allgemeine deutsche Biographie*, XXII (Leipzig, 1885), 686.

[5] Quoted from the introduction to the critical edition of Müller's works: James Taft Hatfield, ed. *Gedichte von Wilhelm Müller, vollständige kritische Ausgabe*, Series Deutsche Literaturdenkmale des 18. und 19. Jahrhunderts No. 137, Dritte Folge, No. 17 (Berlin: B. Behr's Verlag, 1906) pp. xxv-xxvi.

[6] Kerner's account of his investigations into the inner life of his famous patient will be found in: Justinus Kerner, *Die Seherin von Prevorst. Eröffnungen über das innere Leben des Menschen und über das Hereinragen einer Geisterwelt in die unsere* (Stuttgart, 1877).

[7] Artemis-edition (Zürich, 1950), XXIII, 515. There is confusion as to the dating of Müller's visits with Goethe. Cf. Hatfield, *Gedichte von Wilhelm Müller*, p. xxx.

[8] *Hallesche Literaturzeitung*, No. 7 (January 1825). Reference from Hatfield, op. cit., p. xxxi.

I

[1] Bruno Hake, "Wilhelm Müller. Sein Leben und Dichten" (Diss. Berlin, 1908). Only Chapter 4 was published: *Die schöne Müllerin* (Berlin, 1908).

[2] Cf. in addition to Hake, Philip S. Allen, "Wilhelm Müller and the German Volkslied."

[3] Cf. Hake, op. cit., p. 14.

[4] The text upon which our study is based is the critical edition of James Taft Hatfield (cf. *Introduction*, note 5). Numbers in parentheses following the title of each poem refer to the pages on which the poem will be found in the Appendix.

[5] Cf. Allen, "Wilhelm Müller and the German Volkslied," JEGP, III (1901), 78-79.

[6] Just ("Wilhelm Müllers Liederzyklen") examines the levels of irony involved in the workings of the "lyrisches Ich" in Müller's *Waldhornistenlieder* (of which "Die schöne Müllerin" forms a part) with great sensitivity. Noting that a composer lies hidden within every romantic poet, a fact which causes a certain painful rift within his nature, Just continues: "...die schmerzliche Doppelheit erträgt er nur, wenn er sein Schicksal als Spiel nimmt, wenn er sich in eine Rolle hineinversetzt, kurz: wenn er sich fiktionalisiert. Das ist bei Wilhelm Müller eindeutig der Fall. Auf diese Weise *ist* er und ist er zugleich *nicht* der im Titel genannte Waldhornist, also ein Musiker." (p. 459). In the same study Just later quite correctly points to instances in which the author's treatment of metaphor in "Die schöne Müllerin" occasions the expansion of his use of the lyrical "I" to encompass the widest possible spectrum of individualities: "Von Raumfügung und Farbgebung her erscheint das lyrische Ich als stellvertretend für jeden Menschen." (p. 466).

[7] Just points here to the falling quality of the dactylic handling of lines 2-4 of stanza 3 and underscores the inexorable compulsion to wander on into the depths as this is felt by the lyrical "I" borne along by the flow of *time* ("Zeitfluß"). Ibid., p. 463.

[8] In the following poem ("Halt," 119) the feelings of joy called forth by the sunshine which floods the scene prompt the miller's lad to ask his "brook" the almost rhetorical question (which is really an affirmation of his joy at "finding his way" to the miller's daughter): "War es also gemeint?" Once again Müller's musical sensitivity is evident in the bridge he casts by repeating this last line of "Halt!" as the first line of the following poem "Danksagung an den Bach." This is entirely in keeping with the feelings of elation which carry the boy forward.

Further questions put to the brook ("Danksagung an den Bach") remain unanswered, and the boy contents himself with the outcome, however he may have been led: "Was ich such', ist gefunden,/Wie's immer mag sein."

[9] The age of the miller's boy suggests that the appropriate translation of "Müllerin" is "miller's daughter." Thus she is referred to as the *Müllerstochter* in the recent study by K. G. Just ("Wilhelm Müllers Liederzyklen," 460).

¹⁰ Cf. "Liebesaufruf," Hatfield (*Gedichte von Wilhelm Müller*), pp. 125-126, "Rückblick," p. 116, "Frühlingstraum," pp. 121-122.

¹¹ This idealization of the girl appears in heightened form in "Das Mühlenleben" (122). Here the outer situation is once again described as the miller's daughter moves among the young men, chatting and advising them as to details of their tasks. The transforming power exercised by the girl on the young man's emotions is expressed through the reversal of his reactions to the sound of the millwheel. In stanza four he feels the sound as oppressive, for he wishes to break out into the open air and into the proximity of the girl. Once he has seen her, however, the same sounds are experienced at the end of the poem as music: "Und die Räder, Stein' und Stampfen / Stimmen als Begleitung ein." Indeed, they are felt to be performing a jolly dance—a revival of the motifs of the introductory poem "Wanderschaft." The world is entirely reanimated, and the poem ends with a prayer in praise of the realm of the mill—a direct reversal of the situation at the beginning of the poem. The eighth stanza holds the secret of the transformation. Here Müller draws directly on the medieval *minnesang* tradition, portraying the young lady as the "Herrin" to be viewed from a discreet distance and likened to the omnipresent eye of God. Müller's activities as librarian, literary critic, and editor of several volumes of German Baroque literature, made him keenly aware of literary traditions. These he drew upon, consciously weaving them even into such a seemingly naïve poem as this. The miller boy's idealization of the girl thus rises in dramatic intensity as he portrays her as a quasi-divine being whose very presence serves to reanimate and to poeticize the world ("Ei, da mag das Mühlenleben / Wohl des Liedes würdig sein"). The dramatic development of this cyclical "Monodram" is here served by the introduction of emotions which by reason of their obvious exaggeration must contain within them the seeds of their own disillusionment.

¹² Cf. Just, "Wilhelm Müllers Liederzyklen," 464-466.

¹³ This use of the bird and the wind as carriers of the love message, and also the ever recurring motif of the window are well-known in the folksong tradition. Cf. Allen, op. cit., III, 57, 68, 85.

¹⁴ The two foregoing poems, "Morgengruß" and "Des Müllers Blumen" (p. 123-4), represent largely a reworking of the love theme with the introduction of the favorite images: the window, the identification of the girl's eyes now with stars, now with flowers.

¹⁵ Just, op. cit., p. 465.

¹⁶ Hatfield, *Gedichte von Wilhelm Müller*, pp. 273-282.

¹⁷ The introduction here of the green ribbon sets in motion an allegorical-symbolical use of this color which runs through most of the following six poems. It reaches its climax in "Die liebe Farbe" (p. 129) and "Die böse Farbe" (p. 129) where it is supplanted by white, the color of death. In the following poem ("Blümlein Ver-

gißmein", p. 130) the conventional flower-imagery is perverted through the introduction of a black "anti"-flower and the cycle ends with the reintroduction of blue, the color of the girl's eyes and of the heavens.

[18] Hake, "Wilhelm Müller," 42.

[19] Ibid., pp. 15-16.

[20] The motifs of rejection and jealousy are further developed in "Eifersucht und Stolz" (p. 127) as the boy again turns to the brook to give vent to his inner distress. The themes are then again elaborated in "Erster Schmerz, letzter Scherz" (p. 128), in which the lad seeks consolation in music as he plays songs for the children on his pipe. The inspiration is now drawn, however, from the *past* ("Nun singe neue Lieder / Von alter Seligkeit") and the music of the pipe is clearly less resonant than that of the lute. The idyllic scene described by the boy centers around the favorite image of the young girl seated behind the window.

[21] Cf. Just, "Wilhelm Müllers Liederzyklen," 465-466.

[22] Through the introduction of the traditional death-symbols (cypress, rosemary, grave, cross) the bitter irony of the refrain "Mein Schatz hat's Grün so gern" becomes almost unbearable. The medieval *Minnejagd* motif is employed in stanza two in the allegory of the death hunt, another example of Müller's interest in the older German literature.

[23] The hunting horn (cf. "Des Baches Wiegenlied") sounds, and the girl's window, here most vividly a symbol of separation, reverberates sympathetically with the music produced by the fateful hunter.

[24] In the poem "Erster Schmerz, letzter Scherz" a revengeful curse was directed at the hunter, the disturbing influence breaking into the boy's world from without. The hunter was magically to be hurled into the abyss when treading upon rose petals strewn by the miller's boy. Now, however, the object of the curse is the boy himself.

[25] The image of flowers which spring forth under the girl's feet is found in the folksong tradition. Cf. Allen, "Wilhelm Müller and the German Volkslied," III, 50.

[26] Cf. Allen, III, 47, 50, 64, 80.

[27] The latter image is known in the folksong tradition. Cf. Allen, III, 65.

[28] "Epigrammatische Spaziergänge," Hatfield, G*edichte von Wilhelm Müller*, pp. 306 ff. and 350 ff.

[29] A detailed discussion of the nature of Müller's poetic imagination is presented in Chapter IV.

[30] No. I/38, Hatfield, p. 312.

[31] Hatfield, p. 362.

II

[1] Perhaps a musicologist will discover that certain specifically musical

considerations prompted Schubert to rearrange the sequence of the poems.
2. Cf. Just, "Wilhelm Müllers Liederzyklen," 466-469.
3. Ibid., p. 468.
4. These howling dogs are an example of the vigorous attention to detail of which Müller was capable and which is reflected particularly in such prose works as his book *Rom, Römer und Römerinnen* (Berlin, 1820).
5. The motif of tears appears again in "Wasserfluth" (p. 138). In this singularly unsuccessful poem the tears are sent on their way into town, past the girl's house. The whole treatment reduces the function of the stream to a mere receptacle for unstilled passion.
6. Cf. Allen, "Wilhelm Müller and the German Volkslied," II1, 52-53.
7. Hans Brandenburg, "Die Winterreise als Dichtung. Eine Ehrenrettung für Wilhelm Müller," *Aurora. Eichendorff Almanach*, XVIII (1958), 57-62. Quotation, p. 60.
8. Cf. "Gefrorene Thränen," stanza three and "Wasserfluth," stanza four.
9. This poem has recently been treated in some detail in an article by Wolfgang Stechow, "Der greise Kopf. Eine Analyse," *Festschrift für Werner Neuse*, Herbert Lederer and Joachim Seyppel, eds. (Berlin, 1967), pp. 65-67.
10. Just, "Wilhelm Müllers Liederzyklen," 469.
11. Flowers in winter are a *topos* for that which is impossible. Cf. Allen, "Wilhelm Müller and the German Volkslied," III, 47.
12. Just, p. 471.
13. Ibid., p. 471.
14. Ibid., p. 470.
15. Ibid., p. 471.
16. Ibid., p. 466.

III

1. Letter to Adelheid Müller, June 4th 1824. Philip S. Allen and James Taft Hatfield, *Diary and Letters of Wilhelm Muller* (Chicago, 1903), pp. 119-123.
2. Cf. the letter to Adelheid, June 7th 1824. Ibid., pp. 123-127.
3. Ibid., p. 124.
4. Gustav Schwab, *Vermischte Schriften von Wilhelm Müller*, 5 vols. (Leipzig, 1830), I, p. xxxix.
5. The poem "Morgenlied" (p. 152) reworks this theme of awakening in images which are not imbued with deeper meaning. It contains the usual window-situation, this time with the poet on the inside and the personified morning breeze rapping with a branch on the panes to call him out into nature. The Anacreontic teasings of the sunbeams

and the hoarse nightingale are a bit of eighteenth-century baggage, and the poem ends on a motif well-known to Müller from his medieval studies: *carpe diem* ("Heraus, heraus in des Frühlings Reich! / Es wird nicht lange mehr bleiben").

[6] The poem "Das Brautkleid" (p. 154) picks up the theme of "Die Brautnacht" but develops it in terms of a dry allegory which is alleviated only by an indelicate twist at the end. The earth and the seasons are personified, and the green dress bestowed upon the earth by the month of May turns yellow with grief at his departure. The earth then is literally "undressed" as the grain is harvested on the meadows and must lie down a naked widow until she is given another dress in the spring. The poem might be termed a benignly erotic witticism.

[7] Vienna, Albertina.

[8] Cf. Hatfield, *Gedichte von Wilhelm Müller*, p. ix.

[9] Allen-Hatfield, *Diary and Letters*, p. 68.

[10] Ibid., p. 84.

[11] A similar intoxication of joy is treated in a very limited way and without religious overtones in "Die Biene." It is an Anacreontic poem in which the bee is seen as a creature whose very work is a living example of the satiety experienced by man in his encounter with the gifts of spring.

[12] Cf. the perennial favorite among Müller's drinking-songs, "Die Arche Noäh" ("Das Essen, nicht das Trinken, / Bracht' uns um's Paradies"), Hatfield, *Gedichte von Wilhelm Müller*, pp. 88-89.

[13] We recall the portrayal of meadow flowers as a metaphor for the white tablecloths in "Das Frühlingsmahl." The flowers appear in the present poem with a different metaphorical connotation.

[14] The reader is referred to the critical edition of Hatfield: "Muscheln von der Insel Rügen," pp. 273-285; "Griechenlieder," pp. 183-234.

IV

[1] Cf. also "Jägers Lust" and "Jägers Leid," Hatfield, *Gedichte von Wilhelm Müller*, pp. 127-128.

[2] Cf. Friedrich Schiller, "Über die ästhetische Erziehung des Menschen in einer Reihe von Briefen," *Sämmtliche Schriften, historisch-kritische Ausgabe*, ed. Karl Goedeke (Stuttgart: Cotta, 1871).

[3] Cf. Schwab, *Vermischte Schriften von Wilhelm Müller*, pp. xli-xlii.

[4] Cf. Hatfield, pp. 238 ff. and 341 ff.

[5] *Rom, Römer und Römerinnen*, 2 vols. (Berlin, 1820).

[6] Hatfield, pp. 273 ff.

[7] Arthur Müller, *Moderne Reliquien* (Berlin, 1845), I, 59.

[8] Cf. Chapter I, p. 19, note 16.

[9] Wilhelm Schneider, *Liebe zum deutschen Gedicht* (Freiburg: Herder, 1960), pp. 114 ff.
[10] This is clearly recognized by Lohre in his discussion of a battle which Müller waged successfully in 1823 against the director of the school at which he was employed. Cf. Heinrich Lohre, *Wilhelm Müller als Kritiker und Erzähler* (Leipzig, 1927), p. 72.
[11] Schwab, *Vermischte Schriften von Wilhelm Müller*, pp. xlviii-l.

Bibliography

Allen, Philip S. and Hatfield, James Taft. *Diary and Letters of Wilhelm Müller.* Chicago, 1903.
Allen, Philip S. "Unpublished Sonnets of Wilhelm Müller," *Journal of English and Germanic Philology,* IV (1902), 1-9.
 Very early sonnets, written in Brussels (1814) and not included in the critical edition of Hatfield.
— "Wilhelm Müller and Italian Popular Poetry," *Modern Language Notes,* XIV, No. 6 (1899), 165-166.
— "Wilhelm Müller and the German Volkslied." Diss. University of Chicago, 1899. Reprinted in *Journal of English and Germanic Philology,* II (1898-99), 283-322; III (1901), 35-91; 431-491.
Allen, Philip S. and Klier, I. M. "Wilhelm Müller und das deutsche Volkslied," *Das deutsche Volkslied,* 28. Jg. (1926), 57-61, 73.
Beutler, Ernst, ed. *Johann Wolfgang Goethe. Gedenkausgabe der Werke, Briefe und Gespräche.* 24 vols. Zürich, 1950.
Brandenburg, Hans. "Die Winterreise als Dichtung. Eine Ehrenrettung für Wilhelm Müller," *Aurora,* XVIII (1958), 57-62.
Francke, O. "Zur Biographie des Dichters Wilhelm Müller," *Mitteilungen des Vereins für Anhaltische Geschichte und Altertumskunde,* 5 (1887), 33-44.
Friedländer, Max. "Die Entstehung der Müllerlieder," *Deutsche Rundschau,* LXXIII (1892-93), 301-307.
Hachtmann, O. "Wilhelm Müller und Wir," *Deutsche Rundschau,* CCXIII (54. Jg., 1927), 70-77.
Hake, Bruno. "Wilhelm Müller, sein Leben und Dichten." Diss. Berlin, July 4, 1908.
 Only Chapter IV published: *Die schöne Müllerin.* Berlin, 1908.
Hatfield, James Taft. "Berichtigung des Datums und Inhalts eines Goetheschen Gesprächs mit Kanzler Friedrich von Müller," *Goethe-Jahrbuch,* XXIX (1908), 184-190.
 Discusses Wilhelm Müller's visit with Goethe. Contains also a letter by Müller from the Weimar archive.
— "The Earliest Poems of Wilhelm Müller," *Publications of the Modern Language Association,* XIII (1898), 250-285.

These are Müller's contributions to the volume *Bundesblüthen* (1815). They are not included in the critical edition of Hatfield.
— ed. *Gedichte von Wilhelm Müller, vollständige kritische Ausgabe.* Series *Deutsche Literaturdenkmale des 18. und 19. Jahrhunderts,* No. 137. Dritte Folge, No. 17, Berlin: B. Behr's Verlag, 1906.
— "Newly-discovered Political Poems of Wilhelm Müller," *Modern Language Review,* I (April 1906), 212-222.
— "The Poetry of Wilhelm Müller," *The Methodist Review,* LXXVII (July 1895), 581-594.
— "Unpublished Letters of Wilhelm Müller," *American Journal of Philology,* CXLII (1903), 121-148.
— "Wilhelm Müllers unveröffentlichtes Tagebuch und seine ungedruckten Briefe," *Deutsche Rundschau,* CX (March 1902), 362-380.
— Review of *Wilhelm Müller als Kritiker und Erzähler,* by H. Lohre. *Modern Language Notes,* XLIII (1928), 564-566.
Just, Klaus Günther. "Wilhelm Müllers Liederzyklen 'Die schöne Müllerin' und 'Die Winterreise,'" *Zeitschrift für deutsche Philologie,* LXXXIII (1964), 452-471. Reprinted in *Übergänge. Probleme und Gestalten der Literatur* (Bern and München: Francke, 1966), pp. 133-152.
Lohre, Heinrich. *Wilhelm Müller als Kritiker und Erzähler.* Leipzig, 1927.
Müller, Arthur. *Moderne Reliquien.* Berlin, 1845.
P. 59, *Mein erstes Sonett.* This poem is not contained in the critical edition of Hatfield.
Müller, Curt, ed. *Gedichte von Wilhelm Müller.* Leipzig, 1894.
Includes a biographical introduction and a preface.
Müller, F. Max. *Alte Zeiten, alte Freunde, Lebenserinnerungen.* Gotha, 1901.
Rellstab, Ludwig. *Biographie Ludwig Bergers.* Berlin, 1846.
Discussion of the origin and development of the poems of" Die schöne Müllerin."
Schneider, Wilhelm. *Liebe zum deutschen Gedicht.* Freiburg: Herder, 1960.
Schwab, Gustav. *Vermischte Schriften von Wilhelm Müller.* 5 vols. Leipzig, 1830.
Biography of the poet in vol. I.
Stechow, Wolfgang. "Der greise Kopf. Eine Analyse," *Festschrift für Werner Neuse,* Herbert Lederer and Joachim Seyppel, eds. (Berlin, 1967), 65-67.
Wahl, Paul. *Wilhelm Müllers Rheinreise von 1827 sowie Gedichte und Briefe.* Dessau, 1931.
Wäschke, H. "Aus Wilhelm Müllers Jugendzeit," *Zerbster Jahrbuch,* X (1914), 56-71.
Wirth, Alfred. "Wilhelm Müller und das Volkslied," *Mitteldeutsche Blätter für Volkskunde,* III (1928), 136-142.
Also printed in *Magdeburger Zeitung* (October 3rd, 10th and 17th,

1927). Also reprinted in *Anhaltische Geschichtsblätter*, 4. Heft (Dessau 1929?), 125-161. Source: *Bibliographie der deutschen Zeitschriftenliteratur*, LXIV (1929), 472. In the *Anhaltische Geschichtsblätter* the article appeared under the title "Studien zu Wilhelm Müller" (Cf. Wahl, p. 112).

Index of First Lines and Titles of Poems *

Adelsinstinkt, 99
Alles will ich nun verlernen, 86-87, *153*.
Am Bach viel kleine Blumen stehn, *124*, 160.
Am Brunnen vor dem Thore, 39-47, *137-138*.
Am Feierabend, 13, *120-121*.
Auf dem Flusse, 48-49, *139*.
Auf einen Todtenacker, 56-58, *143*.
Auf kühlen Bergen, an des Meeres Strande, 107-111.
Bächlein, laß dein Rauschen sein!, 19-21, *125-126*.
Bauer und Edelmann, 99.
Biene, dich könnt' ich beneiden, *155-156*, 163.
Blümlein Vergißmein, 25, *130-131*.
Calderon, 105-106.
Danksagung an den Bach, 13, *120*.
Das Brautkleid, *154-155*, 163.
Das Frühlingsmahl, 79-84, *151*.
Das Irrlicht, 58, *143-144*.
Das Mühlenleben, 13-14, *122-123*, 160.
Das Prisma, 102.

Das Wandern ist des Müllers Lust, 9-10, *118-119*.
Das Wirthshaus, 56-58, *143*.
Dem Prisma gleicht des Dichters Seele, in welcher Freud und Leid sich bricht, 102.
Der beste Narr, 99.
Der Dichter, als Epilog, 134.
Der Dichter, als Prolog, 117-118.
Der du so lustig rauschtest, 48-49, *139*.
Der greise Kopf, 49-51, *140*.
Der Jäger, 23, *127*.
Der Leiermann, 63-65, *146*.
Der Lindenbaum, 39-47, *137-138*.
Der Menschenseele gleich in ihres Leibes Hülle, 33-34.
Der Müller und der Bach, 26-27, *132-133*.
Der Neugierige, 13-14, 21, *121*.
Der Peripatetiker, 86-87, *153*.
Der Reif hatt' einen weißen Schein, 49-51, *140*.
Der stürmische Morgen, 53-54, *142*.
Der Wegweiser, 56, *142-143*.
Der Wind spielt mit der Wetterfahne, 37, *136*.

* Entries refer to the principal discussion of each poem. Titles of poems are italicized. Numbers in italics refer to the text of the poems in the Appendix.

Des Baches Wiegenlied, 27-31, *133-134*.
Des Müllers Blumen, *124*, 160.
Die Biene, *155-156*, 163.
Die böse Farbe, 23-25, *129-130*.
Die Brautnacht, 71-79, *150-151*.
Die Fenster auf, die Herzen auf! 70, *147-148*.
Die Flur hat angezogen, *154-155*, 163.
Die Forelle, 87-88, *154*.
Die Krähe, 51, *140-141*.
Die liebe Farbe, 23-24, *129*.
Die Nebensonnen, 59-60, *144*.
Die Post, 47-48, *138*.
Die Wetterfahne, 37, *136*.
Drei Sonnen sah ich am Himmel stehn, 59-60, *144*.
Drüben hinter'm Dorfe, 63-65, *146*.
Eifersucht und Stolz, *127-128*, 161.
Eine Krähe war mit mir, 51, *140-141*.
Eine Mühle seh' ich blicken, 13, *119-120*.
Ein Licht tanzt freundlich vor mir her, 54-56, *142*.
Einsamkeit, 62, *145*.
Erlösung, 84-86, *152*.
Erstarrung, 37-39, *137*.
Erster Schmerz, letzter Scherz, *128-129*, 161.
Es bellen die Hunde, es rasseln die Ketten, 52-53, *141*.
Es brennt mir unter beiden Sohlen, 49-51, *139-140*.
Es hat geflammt die ganze Nacht, 71-79, *150-151*.
Faul in der Arbeit, fleißig im Beten, 99.
Fliegt der Schnee mir in's Gesicht, 62-63, *146*.
Form und Geist, 94.
Fremd bin ich eingezogen, 36-37, *135-136*.
Frühlingseinzug, 70, *147-148*.

Frühlingstraum, 60-62, *144-145*.
Gebet ohne Arbeit, 99.
Gefrorene Thränen, 37, *136*.
Gefrorne Tropfen fallen, 37, *136*.
Gute Nacht, 36-37, *135-136*.
Guten Morgen, schöne Müllerin!, *123-124*, 160.
Gute Ruh', gute Ruh'!, 27-31, *133-134*.
Haben ausgetobt die Stürme, 96-98.
Halt!, 13, *119-120*.
Hätt' ich tausend, 13, *120-121*.
Hier und da ist an den Bäumen, 51-52, *141*.
Ich frage keine Blume, 13-14, 21, *121*.
Ich hört' ein Bächlein rauschen, 10-13, *119*.
Ich lad' euch, schöne Damen, kluge Herrn, *117-118*.
Ich möchte ziehn in die Welt hinaus, 23-25, *129-130*.
Ich schnitt' es gern in alle Rinden ein, 14-15, *123*.
Ich such' im Schnee vergebens, 37-39, *137*.
Ich träumte von bunten Blumen, 60-62, *144-145*.
Ihr Blümlein alle, 25-26, *131-132*.
Im Dorfe, 52-53, *141*.
In der hellen Felsenwelle, 87-88, *154*.
In die tiefsten Felsengründe, 58, *143-144*.
In Grün will ich mich kleiden, 23-24, *129*.
Juli, 107-111.
Kannst du ohne Erdenbild himmlischen Verstand verstehen, 94.
Keine Reis' auf Erden scheint mir so groß und schwer zu sein, 33-34.
Kinderfrühling, 70-71, *148-149*.
Kinderlust, 71, *149-150*.

Letzte Hoffnung, 51-52, *141*.
Manche Thrän' aus meinen Augen, *138-139*, 162.
Mein!, 19-21, *125-126*.
Meine Laute hab' ich gehängt an die Wand, 21-22, *126*.
Meine Muse liebt das Reisen, 90-91, *156-157*.
Memento Mori, 100.
Mit dem grünen Lautenbande, 22-23, *126-127*.
Morgengruß, *123-124*, 160.
Morgenlied, *152-153*, 162-163.
Muth!, 62-63, *146*.
Narren giebt's überall auf der Welt, 99.
Nun feget aus den alten Staub, 71, *149-150*.
Nun merk' ich erst, wie müd' ich bin, 58-59, *144*.
Nun sitz' am Bache nieder, *128-129*, 161.
O heilige Frühlingswonne, 88-90, *156*.
Pause, 21-22, *126*.
Pfingsten, 88-90, *156*.
Rast, 58-59, *144*.
Rath und That, 98.
Rückblick, 49-51, *139-140*.
Schad' um das schöne grüne Band, 22-23, *126-127*.
Seh' ich sie am Bache sitzen, 13-14, *122-123*, 160.
Selbstbeschauung, 96-98.
Springst du freudig durch die Thüre in dein neugebautes Haus, 100.
Täuschung, 54-56, *142*.
That und Wille, 33-34.
Thränenregen, 15-19, *125*.
Tiefe und Klarheit, 113.
Trockne Blumen, 25-26, *131-132*.
Ungeduld, 14-15, *123*.
Viele lange Jahr' es währt, 87.
Von der Straße her ein Posthorn klingt, 47-48, *138*.

Wanderschaft, 9-10, *118-119*.
Wappen ließ die edle Dame in des Säuglings Windeln nähen, 99.
War es also gemeint, 13, *120*.
Was er weiß, macht ihn heiß, 87.
Was in der Menschenseele dunklen Tiefen, 105-106.
Wasserfluth, *138-139*, 162.
Was sucht denn der Jäger am Mühlbach hier?, 23, *127*.
Was treibt mich jeden Morgen, 25, *130-131*.
Was vermeid' ich denn die Wege, 56, *142-143*.
Weil gern man schließt mit einer runden Zahl, *134*.
Wenn der Bauer wird ein Edelmann, 99.
Wer hat die weißen Tücher, 79-84, *151*.
Wer jeder That sich unterfängt, der kömmt zu keinem Rath, 98.
Wer schlägt so rasch an die Fenster mir, *152-153*, 162-163
Wie dem Fische wird zu Muth, 84-86, *152*.
Wie eine trübe Wolke, 62, *145*.
Wie hat der Sturm zerrissen, 53-54, *142*.
Wie hell und klar auch sei der Himmel, du kannst doch seinen Grund nicht sehn, 113.
Wir saßen so traulich beisammen, 15-19, *125*.
Wo ein treues Herze, 26-27, *132-133*.
Wohin?, 10-13, *119*.
Wohin so schnell, so kraus, so wild, mein lieber Bach?, *127-128*, 161.
Wollt euch nicht so schnell belauben, 70-71, *148-149*.
Xenion, 90-91, *156-157*.
Zwei Reisen, 33-34.